No Experience Necessary

Unit One: Help Wanted

Kelly A. Fryer

No Experience Necessary
Bible Study
Unit One: Help Wanted

The No Experience
Necessary Bible study
series was developed
in cooperation with the
Division for Congrega-
tional Ministries (DCM),
Evangelical Lutheran
Church in America.
Thank you to DCM for
its support in helping to
provide sample copies
of Unit One to synod
assemblies in 2005.

Editors:
Gloria E. Bengtson
Laurie J. Hanson
Eileen K. Zahn

Series logo, cover,
and interior design:
Marti Naughton

Cover and interior
images:
BananaStock
Brand X Pictures
Comstock
Digital Vision Inc.
Dover Publications
Photodisc

HELP WANTED

ISBN 0-8066-4810-4

Manufactured in U.S.A.

1 2 3 4 5 6 7 8 9 0 1 2 3 4 5 6 7 8 9 0

Everybody's welcome!

Welcome to the No Experience Necessary Bible study series! It doesn't matter if this is your first or 101st Bible study. No Experience Necessary is designed to be accessible for people new to Bible study and full of fresh insights for others.

Everybody's welcome. No roadblocks. No jargon. No experience necessary.

God's speaking.

Right here. Right now. That's the radically simple assumption at the heart of this Bible study. What's God saying to you? What's God saying to us?

Come as you are.

You can read. You've got common sense. You've got your own experiences. Well, here's the Bible. Off you go. Anyone can be a facilitator for this Bible study too. No special knowledge needed.

You decide.

Many Bible studies tell you what to do. Not this one. No Experience Necessary starts with you. What you think, what you bring to the table, what works best for your group. Yes, there's plenty of support and relevant information in every session. But you choose what to do with it, what works best for your group.

Expect change.

Things are going to happen. The Spirit's at work. You'll never be the same. That's the expectation of this Bible study. Because when you engage God's Word, things change. For you. For your congregation. For the world.

God is on a mission

In No Experience Necessary, you'll open up the Bible and read it for yourself. The most important part of the Bible study is reading from the Bible, listening for God's voice, and talking about what you've read and heard.

As you read the Bible with your small group, you'll see that God has a plan. From the very beginning, God's been

on a mission to save and bless the world. We're called to be partners in this mission. God's got work for us to do—work that gives meaning and purpose to our lives.

In each No Experience Necessary Bible study unit, we'll explore the Bible in light of God's mission. "Help Wanted" (Unit One) shows the broad sweep of what God's been doing. But notice that the unit begins at the very heart of God's mission—with Jesus.

Help Wanted: Unit One

Jesus is at the center of God's mission to save and bless the world. We are called to be partners in that mission. That is the purpose of the Christian life...and our life, together, as the church.

Units Two, Three, and Four take a deeper look into the Bible and the call to be partners with God and each other in God's mission in the world.

SESSION	TITLE	KEY THEME	PRIMARY BIBLE EMPHASIS
1	Job orientation	God is on a mission!	Luke 4:14-44
2	First day on the job	We have been created to be God's partners in this mission.	Genesis 1
3	Making partner	God has a plan to bless the world and invites us to be part of it.	Genesis 11:27—12:9
4	On-the-job training	God's plan is carried out by ordinary people like us.	Exodus 1:1—2:10
5	A human resource problem	Sometimes God has to carry out the plan *in spite of* us.	1 Samuel 8
6	Contract renewal	This partnership really is for better or for worse.	Isaiah 1:1—2:5
7	Working together	Being in partnership with God means being in partnership with one another.	Acts 1:1—2:21

You're Hired: Unit Two

The purpose of our lives (and our life together) is directly connected to God's multifaceted, multidimensional, utterly holistic mission in the world. In other words, we are talking about being part of a very BIG project!

On the Job Training: Unit Three

The purpose of the Christian life is to participate in God's mission in the world. This life will be shaped by a set of particular faith practices.

More Than Just a Job: Unit Four

The purpose of our life together is to participate in God's mission in the world. This purpose shapes the way we do everything we do as the church.

Check these out

Be sure to check out other resources in this series:

- *No Experience Necessary: Everybody's Welcome* (Augsburg Fortress, 2005), a revised and expanded edition of the book by Kelly A. Fryer that inspired the Bible study series.
- *No Experience Necessary: Everybody's Welcome Intro VHS/DVD* (Augsburg Fortress, 2005), a video introduction by Kelly A. Fryer, the series author.
- No Experience Necessary Web site (www.noexperiencenecessary.org), a place to find the latest information and order series resources.

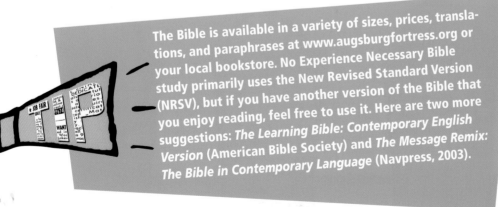

The Bible is available in a variety of sizes, prices, translations, and paraphrases at www.augsburgfortress.org or your local bookstore. No Experience Necessary Bible study primarily uses the New Revised Standard Version (NRSV), but if you have another version of the Bible that you enjoy reading, feel free to use it. Here are two more suggestions: *The Learning Bible: Contemporary English Version* (American Bible Society) and *The Message Remix: The Bible in Contemporary Language* (Navpress, 2003).

Making your group work

You are being invited to answer God's call to follow Jesus into a life that is different...a life that makes a difference in the world.

This is a pretty big deal. And so, although you could do this Bible study by yourself, you might want to consider doing it with a few friends. In a small group, you'll have opportunities to get to know each other, learn from each other, and support each other.

A No Experience Necessary small group can get going with as few as two or three people who want to learn from the Bible and each other. A congregation might start several groups at once or begin a No Experience Necessary Bible study with a group that already exists (for example, a new member class, a women's group, a men's group). However your group comes together, if you have more than a dozen people, consider forming two smaller groups so everyone has a chance to talk.

Making a group work takes a team effort.

A team effort

Making a group work takes a team effort. If you are doing this Bible study with others, here's how to help your group to work:

- Think about people you know—family members, friends, neighbors, coworkers—and invite someone to join your group.
- Pray for the group and everyone in it.
- Attend group meetings regularly and bring a Bible if you have one.
- Do your "homework" between sessions, if your group chooses to do this.
- Respect others in the group and make them feel welcome.
- Keep confidential information inside the group.
- Remember that everybody in the group has something to offer.

You'll learn from the Bible and each other.

Facilitators

Every No Experience Necessary group needs a facilitator to encourage discussion and make sure everyone feels welcome. One person might facilitate the group for an entire unit or your group might rotate leadership each week.

The facilitator isn't expected to be an expert. In fact, it's the facilitator's job to NOT be the expert in the discussion. Everybody has something to offer, but people won't offer it if they're looking to one person for all the "right" answers.

If you are a facilitator in No Experience Necessary, here are additional ways that you help your group to work:

- Tell others about your group and invite them to join. Be sure to let them know when and where you are meeting.
- Make group meetings a high priority.
- Distribute the No Experience Necessary Bible study and *No Experience Necessary: Everybody's Welcome* book to the group.
- Read each session, including the main Bible passage and "Group Tips," ahead of time. "Group Tips" gives you suggestions for leading your group through the material.
- Make sure your group has a relaxed and inviting place to meet with good lighting, plenty of seating, and light refreshments if you choose. Arrange chairs in a circle, if at all possible, so group members can see and hear each other. Ask everyone to turn off cell phone ringers during the sessions.
- Allow time for questions.
- Give everyone a chance to talk without making anyone feel like she or he has to talk or allowing one person to do all the talking.
- Don't do it all. Give members of your group opportunities to set up chairs, talk, pray out loud, read, choose what to do next, make coffee, bring cookies, and so on. Everyone has something to offer.
- Encourage the group to have fun!
- Remind the group why it's there—to open up the Bible and read it together, discover what God is doing in the passage, and listen for what God has to say. That's the main focus for every session.

More resources for facilitators

- Read all of "Everybody's Welcome" (pages 4-7) and "Making Your Group Work" (pages 8-15) as an introduction to the Bible study and your role.
- Read the book *No Experience Necessary: Everybody's Welcome* (Augsburg Fortress, 2005) for more background on what the Bible is about and the ideas behind the Bible study.
- Visit the No Experience Necessary Web site at www.noexperiencenecessary.org for the latest information on the series.
- Remember that everyone has something to offer. You will learn from the Bible and also from the people in your group.
- Rely on the Holy Spirit to guide and challenge you and your group as you listen for God's voice together.

How to get the most out of each session

The "Group Tips" throughout each session provide suggestions for using the following session components with your group.

Come as you are

This is a time to get to know one another, make everybody feel welcome, and begin to build trust within the group.

Start each session by checking in with each other. Invite everyone to briefly share how things are going or get conversation started with the suggestions provided in "Group Tips."

After checking in, read the opening paragraph(s) in the "Come As You Are" section, then take time to pray together. Do this on your own or use the prayer provided in the session.

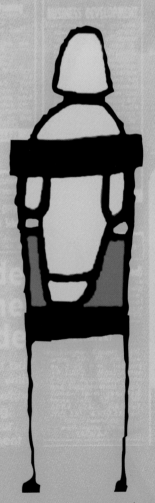

Just 3 questions

Everything in the session builds on the Bible passage and the three questions located here, so be sure to spend the most time on this section every time you meet.

Read the Bible passage out loud and discuss the following questions about the reading.

1|What do you think God is doing here? (In other words, what's going on in this reading? What's God up to? What's the plot of the story? Who are the characters and what are they up to?)

2|What do you hear God saying to you, personally? (What is God saying to you about your life, relationships, work, and so on in this reading? What is God saying to you about what you're called to be or to do?)

3|What do you hear God saying to us (as a small group, congregation, community, nation)? (How is God calling, challenging, directing, forgiving, and loving us in this reading? What is God saying about what we're called to be or to do?)

God is speaking to each one of us, so everyone has something to offer in this discussion. You'll learn from the Bible and each other.

Heart of the matter

This section contains the "lead article" in each session. The lead article draws out themes and gives you additional ways to talk about the main Bible passage.

In "Heart of the Matter," you'll read the lead article and discuss it, using the question(s) found at the end of the article.

Another look; Right to the point; Bible basics; and Right here, Right now

These four sections include "feature articles" that look at the main Bible passage from different angles. Pick one or two of these articles to read, either out loud or to yourself. Then discuss them, using the questions at the end of the articles.

Don't expect your group to get through all of the feature articles included in a session. There are more than enough articles here for your time together, so choose the ones your group is most interested in. (Everyone can read the rest of the articles on their own during the week.)

Get going

No matter how many feature articles you use in the session, close with "Get Going."

Here you'll read the "Wrap Up" article and discuss the question at the end. Then plan for your next meeting. End the session by praying together on your own or use the suggestions provided in this section.

Invite people to join No Experience Necessary.

Exercise your options

You have multiple options in No Experience Necessary, so feel free to use the Bible study in any way that makes sense for your group.

The time and place for your meetings

Most groups find it helpful to have a regular time and place to meet. Meet Sunday mornings at church, Thursday nights with coffee and cookies in someone's home, Saturdays over breakfast in a restaurant, or at another time and place that works for your group.

The length of your sessions

Make sure everyone in the group knows in advance how long the meetings will run. You can meet for 60 minutes, 90 minutes, or for a longer time if the group chooses. Here are suggestions for using your time together.

	60 MINUTES	90 MINUTES	120 MINUTES
Come as you are	10 minutes	15 minutes	15 minutes
Just 3 questions	20 minutes	30 minutes	40 minutes
Heart of the matter	10 minutes	10 minutes	15 minutes
Another look; Right to the point; Bible basics; Right here, right now	15 minutes	30 minutes	40 minutes
Get going	5 minutes	5 minutes	10 minutes

The material covered in your sessions

Focus on reading the main Bible passage and discussing the three questions. Then read the lead article and talk about it. If you have time, read and discuss as many feature articles as you want.

Every person involved in the Bible study should have *No Experience Necessary: Everybody's Welcome* (Augsburg Fortress, 2005). Decide how you'll use the book as a group. You can decide to read a couple of chapters during the course of each Bible study unit or, if you wish, read the entire book at once and refer back to it during each unit. Discuss the book in your regular meetings or schedule an extra meeting or two to talk only about the book.

"Homework" done between sessions

As everybody in the group gets more and more involved in discussion, you'll probably find that each session contains more feature articles than you can cover in one meeting. That's great! Read the rest of the articles on your own during the week. If you want, you can talk about what you've read as you check in at the next meeting. Or decide as a group to read the main Bible passage or one of the articles for the next session in advance. Of course, your group also has the option to not do any homework between sessions.

The *No Experience Necessary: Everybody's Welcome Intro* VHS or DVD (Augsburg Fortress, 2005)

Schedule a special "kickoff" meeting for your group to view the VHS or DVD and learn about the series. If your congregation is starting more than one No Experience Necessary group, you might hold a combined "kickoff" for members of all the groups. Also, consider using the video to invite people to join No Experience Necessary:

- Show all or part of the video before or after worship or at other gatherings in your congregation.
- Loan the video to friends and neighbors and invite them to join your group.
- Invite members of your congregation and community to a "No Experience Necessary Night" and encourage people to bring their friends, family members, neighbors, and coworkers. Set up tables and place a sign-up form for No Experience Necessary groups on each one. After a light supper or snack, show the video and then spend some time in discussion.

TIP

Whether or not you have read and studied the Bible before, watch for "Tips" like this one. They will help you read and interpret Bible passages on your own.

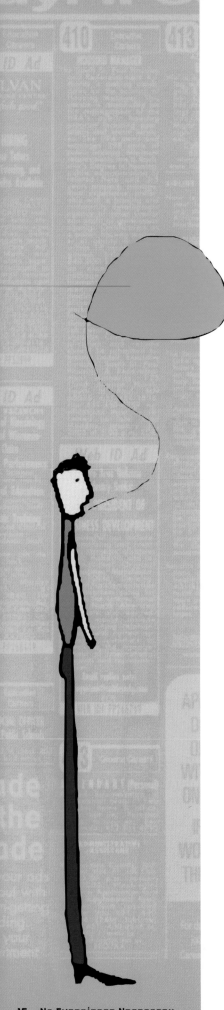

A Letter from the writer

If you've looked for a job recently, you may have checked out the organization's Web site before you filled out an application or asked around before you went in for an interview. You tried to find out everything you could about the organization or the boss, and the people who work there. You wanted to know what they were up to, and whether it seemed like there was a place for you there.

Well, God doesn't exactly have a Web site. But God *has* given us the Bible.

In the Bible, we meet a God who is on a mission to bless the world and who calls us to be a part of that adventure. We also meet a lot of other people just like us, who are extraordinarily gifted and all messed up, at the same time. Weirdly enough, God wants *our* help. You see, God loves us! God loves us and wants our lives to make a difference and mean something. God wants to put us to work.

> In the Bible, we meet a God who is on a mission to bless the world and who calls us to be a part of that adventure.

This Bible study is for people who want to answer God's call to get to work doing something that really matters. *No experience is necessary.* And everybody is welcome. But you will have to be prepared to learn a lot, give a lot, change a lot. Doing this Bible study is part of that. But don't for a second think the work stops here.

God loves us and wants our lives to make a difference and mean something.

The whole point of Bible study is transformation. God wants to change our lives—yours and mine—so through us, God can change the world. We are invited to answer God's call to follow Jesus into a life that is different...and a life that makes a difference in the world.

In "Help Wanted," this first unit of No Experience Necessary, we'll get to know this wonderful God who wants our help. Each of the seven sessions draws us deeper into the story of God's mission, beginning "in the beginning" with the book of Genesis. Then we make our way through some of the peak moments in this story: the promise to Abraham and Sarah; the call of Moses; the mess we made when we wanted a king; the restoration promised by the prophets; the coming of *the* King; and the sending out of the disciples with good news.

This Bible study is going to really make a difference only if you are in the Bible digging around, asking questions, and listening for what God has to say to you through these words. So at every point, you'll be invited to open up your Bible and read it for yourself. Everything else is secondary, although it might help get you thinking, spark your imagination, or challenge you to look at things differently.

Maybe you have been invited to join a group somebody else is starting or maybe your congregation is getting a lot of No Experience Necessary small groups started up at once. If there isn't a No Experience Necessary group to join, go ahead and start one.

Think about who you know who might be willing to do a No Experience Necessary Bible study with you. They don't have to be members of your congregation...or any congregation! Invite your neighbors, friends, coworkers, family members—anybody who can't resist the idea that God wants to put them to work.

Come on. Do it. It'll be fun.

Kelly A. Fryer

God is on a mission!

1 | JOB ORIENTATION

COME AS YOU ARE

God is up to something! And everything we know about it begins with Jesus Christ. In Jesus, we get a glimpse of God's *mission* in the world. So let's take a peek. We meet Jesus here in Luke's Gospel at the very beginning of his public ministry. And we find him in a synagogue, a Jewish house of worship! Now there were synagogues everywhere in Jesus' day. And while a priest had to be present for religious activities in the temple in Jerusalem, the people took turns leading in a synagogue. Someone prayed. Someone read from the scriptures. Someone gave a sermon. Someone made sure a collection was taken for the poor. Today, it was Jesus' turn to help lead. He picked a passage from the book of the prophet Isaiah. He opened it up. And he *changed history*. Forever.

Spend some time getting to know one another. Then take some time to pray together. You can do this however you want, or pray the following prayer out loud.

Dear God, thanks for bringing us together. As we study the Bible, help us learn from each other. Help us listen for your voice. In Jesus' name. Amen

JUST 3 QUESTIONS

Read Luke 4:14-44 out loud, with everyone who is willing taking a turn reading a verse or two at a time. Then spend some time answering these three questions about the reading.

1 | **What do you think God is doing here?**

2 | **What do you hear God saying to you, personally?**

3 | **What do you hear God saying to us (as a small group, congregation, community, nation)?**

GROUP TIPS

"Group Tips" provides suggestions for doing this Bible study with a small group. Be sure to also read pages 4-17 for more on this.

If your group doesn't already have a facilitator, choose one now or rotate this role with each session.

COME AS YOU ARE

Spend time getting to know one another. You might take turns answering this question: "How'd you get your first job?"

You will begin every session by praying together. This might be new for some group members, but they won't be asked to do something they're not ready for.

JUST 3 QUESTIONS

Here you'll read the main Bible passage for the session and discuss three questions. This is the heart of the Bible study series!

When your group discusses these questions, there aren't any experts or "right" answers. Everybody can bring something helpful, insightful, and true to this conversation.

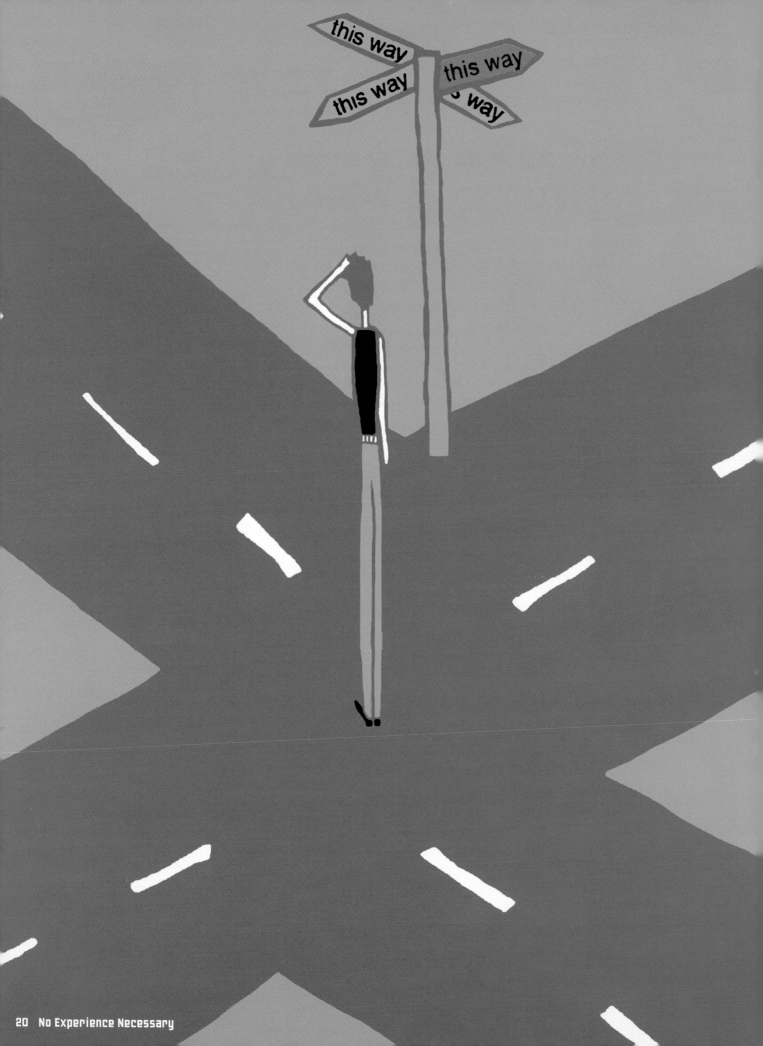

The place to start

HEART OF THE MATTER

This section of the Bible study contains the "lead article" in each session. These lead articles draw out themes and give you additional ways to discuss the main Bible passage.

Spend some time quietly reading through the "Heart of the Matter" article titled "The Place to Start." Then take a few minutes to talk about it. The questions at the end of the article might help you get the conversation started.

So you're ready to get to work doing something that really matters with your life. Or maybe you've been at it for awhile but it's time for you to re-up, recommit, reenergize. And because you're so eager to get going, this may sound strange. But the place to start is *not* with you. Rather, a discussion about the meaning and purpose of our lives has to begin with *God*.

Adventure in progress

You see, God is up to something! From the beginning of creation, in fact, *God has been on a mission to love and bless this world*. If God's mission was a train, you might say that it has already left the station. If it was a NASCAR race, you could tune in to see a live leader board. The crowd, up on its feet, would be drowned out by the sound of screaming engines. If it was an important package being shipped across the world, you could log on and track its progress, only to find that it is already well on its way.

This adventure is *already* in motion. It started long, long, *long* before we were around.

But that doesn't mean it's too late for us. In fact, God's mission includes inviting *people like us* to get involved. That starts with discovering what God is up to so we can answer the call to jump on board.

> God's mission includes inviting people like us to get involved.

And discovering what God is up to begins with *Christ*.

That's why this Bible study doesn't begin at the beginning of the Bible. We'll get to the rest of the Bible soon enough. And God will have something to say to us there, in every book, every passage, every word. But here, in this Bible study, we are starting with the story of Jesus.

The big deal

Notice that the first word Jesus speaks after reading the scripture is "today" (Luke 4:21). "Today," Jesus said, "something has happened that has

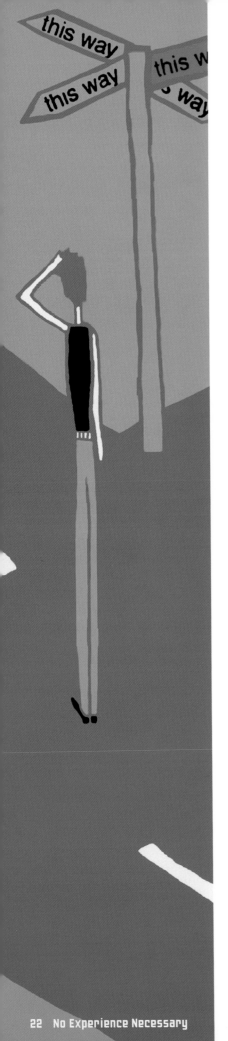

This good news is. . .for the whole world. It isn't just for those who think like us or look like us or act like us.

never happened before. Everything you ever dared to hope for has arrived. Today, God has come to you."

You see, when Jesus appeared, preaching and teaching and healing and announcing that a new king was in town, *God showed up!* Lives were changed. Jesus not only came announcing the "kingdom of God" (4:43), in him we can *see* what this new kingdom looks like. We get a glimpse, in other words, of what God is planning for us and for our world. And we see clearly that this is what God has been up to all along. In Jesus Christ we have the clearest picture of who God is, what God is doing, and how God goes about doing it. Jesus stands at the very center of God's mission in this world. And his message couldn't have been clearer:

> *This is God's world. God is at work in it. God will stop at nothing to save it. God loves it.*

Furthermore, this good news is *for every place* (4:43). It is to be declared in the public spaces we occupy (4:31-37) and it reaches into our most private ones (4:38-39). This good news is *for everyone*: the tortured (4:35) and the sick (4:39) and the searching (4:42). It is, above all, for people on the edges of life: the poor and the oppressed and those victimized by injustice (4:18-19). This good news is, in other words, *for the whole world*. It isn't just for those who think like us or look like us or act like us. The message Jesus brings is radical in the way it reaches out to include absolutely everyone.

This is, in fact, what got Jesus into so much trouble that day in the synagogue (4:16-30). Jesus' listeners weren't too happy about the idea that his good news wasn't just for *them*. (Consider this fair warning that following Jesus may lead

you into places you don't want to go and will almost always lead to trouble.)

Climb aboard

When Jesus appeared, God showed up! In Jesus, we have the clearest picture of God's mission to love and bless the world. Strangely perhaps—and wonderfully!—this mission includes inviting people like us to participate.

Based on what you know about Jesus, what is God like? How would you describe what God is "up to"? What excites (or scares) you about being part of that?

An unexpected invitation

Just in case you're thinking that Jesus intended to carry out his mission all by himself, keep reading. In fact, go ahead and *read Luke 5:1-11* right now.

The way Luke tells this story, Jesus announces, "It's my job to take the good news of God's kingdom to everybody! That's why I came." The very next thing he does is to find himself some partners.

Unlikely partners

And what partners they are! They didn't know who they were dealing with, exactly. They could see that Jesus was a good teacher and a very powerful person. But they wouldn't figure out who Jesus really was for a long while yet.

Even so, Peter knew enough to confess, "Go away! I don't deserve to have you talking to me!" Peter had done all kinds of things he was embarrassed about. He was a sinner and he knew it.

And yet Jesus not only talked to Peter, he invited him to be part of the adventure. "From now on, Peter, you're with me. And together we're going to catch a lot of people."

"Come on," Peter must have thought, "I'm not even very good at catching fish." Under his breath, he might have added, "As you have noticed."

That day, Peter and his friends all dropped what they were doing to follow Jesus.

It's all in the call

Today some of us are used to thinking about these guys as saints. But the truth is, they were just people a lot like us. Messed up and scared half to death. No special training or fancy degree program proving their readiness to be key players in God's mission. What made them ready to follow Jesus was simply this: Jesus invited them. He called them. And that invitation, that *call*, comes to us all.

In fact, we'll hear more about this call from Luke at the end of this unit when we read from the second book he wrote. That book is called Acts.

When have you heard a "call" to do something that really mattered? Did you realize at the time that this was a call from Jesus?

GROUP TIPS

In each session, the lead article is followed by four "feature article" sections: "Another Look," "Right to the Point," "Bible Basics," and "Right Here, Right Now."

Look through the feature articles and pick one or two that look interesting. This is entirely up to your group. Let the Spirit guide your choice! Read the articles either out loud or to yourself. Then talk about them. Use the discussion questions to get your conversation going.

Don't feel like your group has to get through all of these articles. Encourage group members to read the rest of the articles on their own during the week.

ANOTHER LOOK

If you choose this article, you'll read and discuss another portion of the Bible that sheds light on the main Bible passage.

Have everyone who is willing take turns reading Luke 5:1-11.

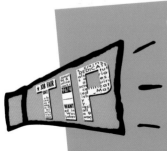

In every way, the story of Jesus is a continuation of the Old Testament story that includes Abraham and Sarah, Moses and Miriam, Samuel and David and Isaiah (all people we'll meet as we go). Jesus came *for* the whole world. But it's important to remember, too, that he came *from* the people of Israel. (That's why the reading for this session starts out with Jesus in a synagogue, reading from Isaiah.)

Backwards and upside down

Martin Luther said that humility is one of the main characteristics of the Christian life. No wonder! As the story of Jesus' life moves along in Luke's Gospel, we see a strange pattern developing. Our expectations keep getting turned upside down. *Read Luke 9:18-23* for the biggest shock of all.

A strange story

This is how things go in Luke's Gospel: We expect the people of Nazareth to welcome Jesus with open arms and, instead, they chase him out of town (Luke 4:28-29). We expect Jesus, who we know is the Lord, to gather the smartest, most powerful people he can find to help him with his mission. Instead, he collects the most unlikely group of followers (5:3-11, 27-28). We expect the religious leaders, the ones who read the Bible and pray a lot, to be the ones to recognize Jesus. They don't. In fact, they argue with him (5:30). Eventually, they are ones who plot to have him killed (22:1-2).

> This is a wonderful but, nevertheless, very strange God. This is a God who chooses the unlikely and loves the unlovable. This is a God whose loving arms stretch out to embrace the world...from a cross.

And that, of course, is the most unexpected thing of all. Peter finally recognizes Jesus for who he really is, the Messiah or "anointed one" of God (9:20). But Jesus turns out to be a very different kind of messiah. He didn't come to rule over the world with force, killing off his enemies and securing his borders. He came to give himself away, to suffer and die even, for the sake of everyone...even his enemies. He came to tear down the borders that divide people from God and from each other. He came in love. And those who follow him are called to do the same.

A strange God

If in Jesus we catch a glimpse of who God is, then we have to conclude: This is a wonderful but, nevertheless, very strange God. This is a God who chooses the unlikely and loves the unlovable. This is a God whose loving arms stretch out to embrace the world... from a cross. And that is the strangest thing of all. The God of the universe could have chosen any other way. Let's be honest: if it was any one of us, we would have chosen another way. But instead, God chose scandal and suffering. God chose the way of radical love. God chose the cross. And it is there, on a cross, that we have the clearest picture of who God is and what God is up to.

This is a God who will never let you forget that, although you are called to be God's partner, only God is God. You are not.

Can you think of a time when you were surprised by God? What happened?

Detective work

R eading the Bible can be very straightforward. Read a passage alone or with a group. Ask some questions (for example, "What is God doing here?" and "What do I hear God saying to me here?" and "What do I hear God saying to us?"). And be open to what God is saying to you there. The Bible is God's written "Word." God wants to speak to you through it. Trust that and listen.

Reading the Bible, however, can be an even richer experience when you approach it like a detective. For example, a little investigating would tell you that the first three Gospels have a lot in common. *Compare Luke 9:21-27 with Matthew 16:24-28 and Mark 8:31—9:1.* Because of that, Matthew, Mark, and Luke are often called the "Synoptic Gospels." Synoptic *(sin-op-tick)* is a word that means seeing things the same way.

But don't be fooled.

Although these three Gospels tell many of the same stories, each one was written to a different audience and each has its own point of view. You can sometimes figure out what a story in one of them means by looking at what is different from the way the other two tell it. Are any words missing? Or added? Is what comes right before or right after the story different? *Each of these writers had a reason for telling a story somebody else had already told.* Look for the clues!

Knowing something about the history of what you're reading can be really helpful. Paying attention to how the story you're reading is put together, in order to figure out what the point of it is, can also lead to deeper understanding. (This is known as taking a "narrative" approach to interpretation.) This Bible study favors the narrative approach but is also interested in the historical background of the text, whenever we can figure that out.

The point is, don't be afraid to tackle the Bible even if you are brand new to it and feel like you don't know anything! But don't be afraid, either, to get out your magnifying glass and do a little investigating. Dig deep. Think hard. Learn more.

> **The point is, don't be afraid to tackle the Bible even if you are brand new to it and feel like you don't know anything!**

So read Luke 9:23; Matthew 16:24; and Mark 8:34 one more time. What differences do you notice? What do you make of these?

GROUP TIPS

RIGHT TO THE POINT

If you choose this article, you'll focus on one key thing about God and following Jesus. (See page 23 for more on feature articles.)

Take turns reading Luke 9:18-23.

BIBLE BASICS

If you choose this article, you'll learn more about the Bible and listening for what God is saying through these words.

Take turns reading Luke 9:21-27; Matthew 16:24-28; and Mark 8:31—9:1. How are these passages the same? How are they different?

Bob

> Grace works something like this: It's your first day of school. And you're nervous and shy and feeling completely inadequate. You're wondering whether or not you can cut it when suddenly the teacher walks in, looks you over, and says to the whole class, "You all get As."

The first time I realized how important—and how difficult—it is for us to understand the wonderful message at the center of the Bible came in the middle of my first month on the job. A handful of people were sitting around the table, most of them more scared than I was.

They were sitting there because I was supposed to be teaching them about what it means to be a follower of Jesus. They were new members and, at that church, it was assumed that if you were a "new" one you couldn't possibly know as much as the "old" ones. So I was in the middle of talking about God's grace, which was where they told us in seminary we should always begin.

I was saying that grace works something like this: It's your first day of school. And you're nervous and shy and feeling completely inadequate. You're wondering whether or not you can cut it when suddenly the teacher walks in, looks you over, and says to the whole class, "You all get As." Before you've done or said or accomplished or messed up anything! "Now," the teacher says with a smile, "just do your best." That, I told my class, is sort of what grace is like. God loves you before you even do anything to deserve it.

Now, I didn't make up this example of grace myself, although I can't remember where I first heard it. And it's not the best one I've ever used. In fact, it's really quite ordinary. But when I told that story this time, something wonderful happened.

I looked up across the table and I saw Bob. He was thirty-something, the owner of a moderately successful small business, the father of three. He actually had tears in his eyes. They were piling up on the rim of his eye and threatening to spill over right down his face. In public and all. "What's up, Bob?" I said in my blurt-it-out-and-hope-it-doesn't-backfire sort of way. And he said this: "I don't think I ever knew who God was before" (excerpt from chapter 1 of *No Experience Necessary: Everybody's Welcome*, Kelly A. Fryer, Augsburg Fortress, 2005).

When did you first encounter, in a meaningful way, the good news of Jesus Christ? Who shared this with you?

The Bible is divided into two major sections, the Old Testament and the New Testament. The story of Jesus' life, death, and resurrection is told in the New Testament. And within the New Testament, there are actually four separate books (Matthew, Mark, Luke, and John) that tell this story. They are called *Gospels*, which means "good news."

Wrap up

So we started this Bible study in the middle (actually toward the end) of the Bible! That's not a big deal, is it?

Actually, this is a BIG DEAL. In Luke's Gospel, we meet Jesus. And Jesus is at the very center of God's mission in the world. In him, we get a glimpse of what God is up to and how God goes about doing it. In fact, Jesus is the key to understanding everything that came before him and everything that will come after. Next time, we'll go right back to the beginning to see how this story got started. *Read Genesis 1–2* and come ready for action.

What key ideas are you taking home with you from this session?

End this first session with prayer. You might want to pray the Lord's Prayer together.

**Our Father in heaven,
Hallowed be your name,
Your kingdom come,
Your will be done,
On earth as in heaven.
Give us today our daily bread.
Forgive us our sins
As we forgive those who sin against us.
Save us from the time of trial
And deliver us from evil.
For the kingdom, the power,
and the glory are yours,
Now and forever. Amen**

RIGHT HERE, RIGHT NOW

If you choose this article, you'll read about real people becoming involved in God's mission to bless and save the world. (See page 23 for more on feature articles.)

GET GOING

Read "Wrap Up" out loud or silently, then take turns answering the question.

Be sure everyone knows where and when you're meeting next. As a group, decide what you'd like to do for homework. (For instance, you might read the lead article in the next session.)

As a group, consider reading at least chapters 1–2 in the book *No Experience Necessary: Everybody's Welcome* as you go through this first unit.

End by praying together. There may be some people in your group who are already comfortable praying out loud. But since this is your first session, you might want to pray the Lord's Prayer out loud together.

We have been created to be God's partners in this mission.

2 | FIRST DAY ON THE JOB

COME aS YOU aRE

In this session, we're moving from the very center of the biblical story—Jesus—to the very beginning, as it's described in the book of Genesis. Even if you never picked up a Bible before, you probably know a lot of the stories in the first chapters of Genesis. This is where you find the story of Adam and Eve, the serpent, and the most expensive piece of fruit in history. Cain and Abel are here, in the first-ever family feud. And so is Noah, who had the last laugh when the rain started to fall. Here in Genesis, we get our first glimpse of a God who wants to bless and save the whole world. And we see humans, if you will, in their first day on the job.

Spend some time checking in with each other. Next, feel free to pray in any way that's comfortable for your group. You may want to continue to pray together out loud, at least for a few weeks. If that's the case, try this prayer:

Mighty God, here we are again, ready to hear you speak to us through the words of the Bible. Be in our conversation! Fill up this room with your Spirit. Make us ready to hear your call to be a part of what you are up to. Be at work in our hearts and minds so we can be everything we have been created to be. In Jesus' name. Amen

JUST 3 QUESTIONS

Read Genesis 1 out loud. Take turns reading a verse or two at a time. Then spend some time answering these three questions about the reading.

1 | **What do you think God is doing here?**

2 | **What do you hear God saying to you, personally?**

3 | **What do you hear God saying to us (as a small group, congregation, community, nation)?**
need for companionship
good

GROUP TIPS

Remember, if you are facilitating this group, see pages 4-17 for further suggestions on using this material.

COME aS YOU aRE

Check in with each other in any way that feels comfortable. If you want a jumping-off point for your conversation, try this: "Over the past week or so, did you find yourself thinking about anything you heard during the last meeting? If so, what was it?"

JUST 3 QUESTIONS

The story in Genesis 1 has created a lot of controversy in some congregations and communities over the years. The "theory of evolution" is often pitted against the "theory of creation." Try not to get hung up on those debates. Instead, set those aside for a moment and really try to listen to what God is saying to you. God has something to say to you right now. Open your ears to God's voice!

A job to do

If your group didn't already do this as homework, read the lead article, "A Job to Do," right now. Then take some time to talk about it. Use the question at the end of the article to help you get your conversation started.

These familiar stories in Genesis might be everybody's favorites. But they have caused a lot of trouble too. Some Christians believe the stories in these first chapters are ancient myths, not science or history at all. Other Christians insist these stories (and everything in the Bible) should be read *as history*, as if everything in it happened just the way the Bible says. A lot of Christians *want* to believe things happened the way these stories say they did—or think they *should* believe this—but aren't sure how to make sense of the stories in the context of what they also believe about evolution and the big bang theory.

Just for the moment, let's set these debates aside. Too often they get in the way of actually listening to the stories. And through these stories, God has something to say to us today. These stories are not, first and foremost, about *how* or *when* things happened "in the beginning." These stories are trying to tell us who is responsible for it all—God!—and *why*. They clue us in to what our role is supposed to be. In other words, these stories get right to the point of what life is all about.

> **These stories get right to the point of what life is all about.**

The bottom line

First of all, these old stories in the early chapters of Genesis tell us this is God's world. God made it (Genesis 1:1). And, as messed up as it sometimes seems (Genesis 3; 6; 11), it is a GOOD world (1:31)! The world is good, in part, because God is at work in it. Martin Luther explained God's daily work as the creator this way: "God has created me together with all creatures....In addition, God daily and abundantly provides shoes and clothing, food and drink, house and home, spouse and children, fields, livestock, and all property—along with all the necessities and nourishment for this body and life" (*A Contemporary Translation of Luther's Small Catechism* pocket edition, translated by Timothy J. Wengert, Augsburg Fortress, 1996, page 21).

Second, God has given us a part to play in this world. There is a point and a purpose for our lives! We have been made in God's image (1:26). That means we are partners with God in exercising *dominion* (which means "to have

It is our job to *serve* each other and all creation.

responsibility") "over every living thing that moves upon the earth" (1:28). And *that* means it is our job to *serve* each other and all creation. This is what you and I have been created for.

Third, you and I are NOT God. Ask Adam and Eve (Genesis 3) or the people in Babel (Genesis 11) what happens when you make the mistake of thinking you are! Only God is God. Our desire to BE God, instead of God's partners, is maybe the best definition of *sin* we could come up with. It is a problem we share with all people, from the beginning of time.

Fourth, even when we mess everything up (which we seem to do a lot!), God is faithful (Genesis 9). God never stops loving us. No matter how many times we insist on running away from home. God never stops calling us back...back home...and back to work.

The bottom line is: These stories have caused a lot of trouble for Christians over the years. That's too bad, because they are great stories with a great message. They tell us that from the very beginning, God has been hard at work blessing the world. And we have been created to be partners with God in this wonderful mission.

Debate about the scientific or historical accuracy of these stories if you must. But don't let that prevent you from hearing God's invitation, calling you back home...and urging you to get to work.

You have been made in God's "image." What does that mean to you in your everyday life?

A second story

GROUP TIPS

Pick one or two of the feature articles in this session: "A Second Story," "Who's the Boss?," "Behind the Debates," or "Early Lesson." Read these together out loud or silently. Then talk about them, using the discussion questions to get your conversation going.

Remember, the goal is NOT to get through every article! Encourage group members to read the rest of the articles on their own during the week.

ANOTHER LOOK

If you choose this article, you'll read and discuss another portion of the Bible that sheds light on the main Bible passage.

Have everyone who is willing take turns reading a verse or two from Genesis 2.

Now that you've wrestled a bit with chapter 1 of Genesis, move on and *read Genesis 2*. You'll probably find yourself wondering, as you read, why there seem to be two "creation" stories. Chapter 1 tells us that people were created in God's own image (1:27). No dirt. No rib. No details. Chapter 1 doesn't even say there were *two* people created but, rather, all of humankind (all at once?!). Then suddenly there's a second story in chapter 2, filled with all kinds of colorful details. What's the deal?

It's a dirty job

Well most likely, long before this stuff was written down, there were two stories floating around. Neither was intended to give a historical or scientific account of how or when creation happened. In fact, some scholars tell us that both of these stories were similar to the creation stories told by other ancient tribes back then. But these two stories in the first chapters of Genesis were told in a particular way. You see, they were told by the Israelites, who had a special relationship with God. (You'll hear more about this in Session 3.) When these stories were told, around campfires outside tents under the night sky, God was at work in them. God was at work in them, too, when they were finally written down. And both stories were included because both had important things to communicate about God, the world, and our place in it.

In chapter 1, for example, we meet a God who is creative and powerful...but a little distant. In chapter 2, God's hands get dirty. God is more real. God *breathes*! God wants to have a relationship with people. And, having been made in God's image, we are made to want to be in relationships too. God wants us to have companions in this life...pets (notice, God first brings animals to the human!),

We have been created to be God's partners, and partners with one another.

friends, lovers. We have been created to be God's partners, and partners with one another. It is not good for us to be alone!

Frankly, it's hard to imagine the creation story without chapter 2! And it's not hard to see why those ancient Israelites thought that one story just wouldn't do.

Is there anything you have learned or read so far in this session that really challenges you? Frustrates or confuses you? Excites you? Talk about it.

Chapter 3

Who's the boss?

God is God... and we are not.

Those ancient storytellers had fun naming the main character in this drama. Adam's name in Hebrew is a play on words. "The LORD God," they said, "formed man *(a-dam)* from the dust of the ground *(a-da-mah)*, and breathed into his nostrils the breath of life" (Genesis 2:7). Adam was called into partnership with God from the very beginning. He was given the job of tending the earth (2:15) and caring for God's creatures. He was even asked to name them all (2:19)!

God is God

But now go ahead and *read Genesis 3*. Unfortunately, what we find here is that Adam wasn't satisfied with his job description. He and Eve believed they could—and should—be in charge of things. It wasn't enough for them to be God's partners. They wanted to BE God. And when that serpent came along, his job wasn't even that hard.

"See that tree over there?" it hissed. "That one God said you should leave alone? That's the only one worth eating from. One bite *and you'll be just like God*."

Adam and Eve couldn't resist. Juice dribbled down their chins as they closed their eyes and bit into what they believed would be a fast track to a corner office on the top floor. They thought they'd be running the show. They couldn't have been more wrong.

What they experienced, instead, was the shame of seeing themselves exposed as the frauds they really were. They quickly covered themselves up, embarrassed by their own weakness and afraid of God's rightful wrath (3:7). This is how it turns out every time we try to take matters into our own hands, forgetting that God is God...and we are not.

If you're up to it, tell about a time when you got yourself into trouble by trying to BE God, instead of God's partner.

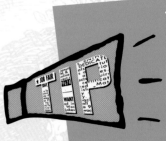

The Bible was written by a lot of different people, over a really long time. Some of the stories in it may be up to 3,000 years old. The Old Testament is the oldest part of the Bible. It tells the story of the Israelites and was originally written mostly in the Hebrew language. The New Testament, which tells the story of Jesus and the earliest Christians, was written mostly in Greek.

Behind the debates

Christians often disagree about things like creation and evolution, marriage and divorce, gender roles and sexual orientation, and other important issues. Different ways of reading and interpreting the Bible are usually behind these disagreements.

It's always dangerous, of course, to create categories. And no one ever fits perfectly under any "label." But just for the sake of comparison, here are some B R O A D categories to help us think about some of the different ways the Bible is often read and interpreted.

- Church leaders and official church teachings interpret the Bible.
- The Bible is interpreted literally.
- The Bible, while not authoritative, is considered a helpful companion to people of faith.
- An attempt is made to discover the "original" meaning of each text by understanding the context (history, culture, theological perspective, and so on) within which it was written.
- The Bible is interpreted from the perspective of people reading it today, particularly those who are poor and oppressed.
- An effort is made to create a lively conversation between the meaning of the biblical text and the world we live in today.

That last description best sums up the approach this Bible study takes. We will use a variety of tools to try to figure out everything we can about the texts we read. We'll ask questions like "Who wrote this?" and "When?" and "What did it mean to the people it was originally written for?" We'll look at the way the texts have been put together, as stories, and think about what the authors might have been trying to say. But we'll also ask, "What does this story have to say to us right now?" and "How is this good news for us today?" We will try to be faithful to the past *and* relevant to the present.

The Word of God comes to us in different ways. First, we hear the *spoken* Word of God in a sermon; or when we are told, during worship for example, that our sins are forgiven; or when a Christian friend assures us, in the midst of troubles, that God loves us and holds us up. Second, there is the *written* Word of God, which we find in the Bible. We turn to this authority in questions of faith and daily life. But finally, and most importantly, there is the *living* Word of God. *The Word of God is Jesus Christ* himself (John 1:1, 14). The living Word, therefore, is at work in the world right now. That's why God's Word could never be confined to words on any page (not even the Bible). The Word of God would survive even if all the Bibles in the world disappeared.

The Bible is one very important way that God speaks to us today. As we read it together, we'll *expect* to hear God's voice. We'll expect to be surprised and challenged, informed and *transformed* by what we hear.

RIGHT TO THE POINT

If you choose this article, you'll focus on one key thing about God and following Jesus. (See page 33, "Group Tips," for more on feature articles.)

Take turns reading Genesis 3.

BIBLE BASICS

If you choose this article, you'll learn more about the Bible and listening for what God is saying through these words.

Think of times when you've heard God speaking to you. Who or what did God use to get through to you?

Early lesson

I learned early on that the purpose of my life had something to do with making this world a better place. I was seven years old. It was 1968, right in the thick of a heated presidential primary season. My dad was talking to Robert F. Kennedy's local campaign manager.

"What do you mean you don't have time to stop here?" he said, snarling into the phone. "You told me Senator Kennedy would be at our house before dark today. My daughter has been waiting for him since 8:00 this morning."

It was true. I had been. I had written a letter to Senator Kennedy some months before, inviting him to my house for "tea" when his campaign made a swing through my town. I don't know what made me think he would come. And I had never even tasted tea before.

We were an ordinary family. My dad worked in a factory. Education was important to my parents but nobody I was related to had ever gone to college. There were a lot of months when we had trouble paying the bills.

"This is exactly what I was afraid would happen," my dad said, growling, "but I am not going to let you send my daughter the message that she doesn't matter. You are going to stop here tonight. And you are going to help my daughter learn that she really can make a difference in this world."

At about 9:00 that night, the street I lived on filled with lights. Camera crews and a crowd of thousands poured into the street, with a white stretch convertible limousine at the center of it all. The car stopped right in front of my house and I heard a strangely familiar voice call my name. I was lifted over the crowd by strangers and lowered into the back seat of the car. Right next to Ethel and Bobby Kennedy.

He smiled at me and I asked him the question I had been waiting all day to ask. "Senator Kennedy, when you're elected president, will you bring my Uncle Bill home from Vietnam?"

His face darkened, serious now. He paused. "With God's help, honey, I'll sure try."

Robert F. Kennedy never got a chance to do what he said he would do. But I never forgot his determination to do the things that really matter.

And, yes, Dad. I hear you too.

> You are going to help my daughter learn that she really can make a difference in this world.

Tell about someone who has been an example of what it means to be God's partner in making this world a better place. For whom are you setting an example?

Wrap up

This is God's world! It is broken, but God has a plan to save and bless it. And *we* have been hired on for the job! We make a mess whenever we try to BE God, instead of being God's partners. But God never, ever stops calling us back home...and back to work.

We see this most clearly in Jesus Christ. But we see it here, too, right at the very beginning of the story...at the beginning of time! Next time, in Genesis 12, we'll meet a couple of people who found themselves right in the middle of God's plan.

What key ideas are you taking home with you from this session?

End the session with prayer. You can use the Lord's Prayer or a prayer of your own. Thank God for being present in your conversation and ask God to bless you in the coming days as you learn more about what it means to be God's partners.

Our Father in heaven,
Hallowed be your name,
Your kingdom come,
Your will be done,
On earth as in heaven.
Give us today our daily bread.
Forgive us our sins
As we forgive those who sin against us.
Save us from the time of trial
And deliver us from evil.
For the kingdom, the power,
and the glory are yours,
Now and forever. Amen

GROUP TIPS

RIGHT HERE, RIGHT NOW

If you choose this article, you'll read about real people becoming involved in God's mission to bless and save the world. (See page 33, "Group Tips," for more on feature articles.)

GET GOING

Read "Wrap Up" out loud or silently. Then go around the group and answer the question at the end of the reading.

Talk about whether there is something you all want to agree to do before the next meeting. How about reading the main Bible passage and the lead article in the next session, for example?

Also consider reading chapter 1 in the book *No Experience Necessary: Everybody's Welcome.*

As a group, choose how to end your time together. You could pray the Lord's Prayer. Or maybe someone is willing to pray out loud, in his or her own words, on behalf of the group.

3|MAKING PARTNER

God has a plan to bless the world and invites us to be part of it.

COME AS YOU ARE

I n Jesus, we meet a God who loves the world and will stop at nothing to save it. We discover in the first chapters of Genesis that God has been at this since the beginning of time. God is on a mission to bring the whole world back home again. Strangely, God chooses to partner with *people* to get this done. And people are proving to be very messy business. As we pick up the story in Genesis 11–12, God is just about to elect two of the messiest people ever to be a part of the plan. Abraham (who consistently acts like he doesn't believe God's promises) and Sarah (who in chapter 18 actually *laughs* at the promises!) are told they will be blessed to be a blessing. This God is full of surprises.

Spend some time checking in with each other. Next, take some time to pray. You can do this however you want but, one way or another, begin with prayer asking God to speak to you during this Bible study time. If you want a prayer to pray together out loud, try this:

Loving God, you are at work in our world and in our lives through the power of your Holy Spirit. Thank you for bringing us together again to study your Word and listen for your living voice. Help us hear the call to love and bless your world, and give us the courage to answer this call. In Jesus' name. Amen

JUST 3 QUESTIONS

Read Genesis 11:27–12:9 out loud. Take turns reading a verse or two at a time. Then spend some time answering these three questions about the reading.

1 | What do you think God is doing here?

2 | What do you hear God saying to you, personally?

3 | What do you hear God saying to us (as a small group, congregation, community, nation)?

Partners in the plan

If your group didn't already do this for homework, take a few minutes to silently read the lead article "Partners in the Plan." Then spend some time discussing it. You may want to use the question at the end of the article for this.

The book of Genesis is grittier than any daytime soap opera or primetime drama. It's got a cast of fascinating characters you can't help but care about—and sometimes can't help but hate! It has a plot of historic proportions and *eye-popping* tales of murder, sex, betrayal, political intrigue, and unfailing love. There is so much going on in this book, in fact, it would be easy to lose track of the main story line: God is on a mission to save and bless the whole world. And, boy, does it need saving.

An early pattern

We knew from the start, with that whole forbidden fruit fiasco in Genesis 3, that things were going to be rough here on earth. It wouldn't matter how lovingly God provides for us or how carefully God points us in the direction of the good life, we would insist on going our own way over and over again. We also knew that there would be some rather dramatic consequences for messing up. Adam and Eve had to pack up and leave the garden. Sin is serious business. But God's faithfulness is more serious still, and Adam and Eve left the garden with a brand new set of clothes (Genesis 3:21). In fact, each and every time we mess things up, God steps in, at just the right time, with a promise of blessing.

> Each and every time we mess things up, God steps in, at just the right time, with a promise of blessing.

This pattern (we do wrong by God, by each other, and by the world...we suffer consequences... God steps in with a blessing...we do wrong...we suffer consequences...God steps in with a blessing...we do wrong...) is repeated again and again in the book of Genesis. The fruit disaster in chapter 3 is followed by the story of Adam and Eve's son, Cain, in chapter 4. Cain kills his brother in a fit of jealousy. He is exiled and sentenced to a life on the run, separated from home and family, but God puts a mark on him so everyone will know not to hurt him. Yes, God even stepped in for Cain.

But the story doesn't stop there. At one point, we're told things got so bad here on earth that only one family on the whole planet was worth saving. They were

In every case, in every story, God answers human sinfulness with love.

related to a guy named Noah who, thankfully, had the good sense to listen when God told him to build a big boat (6:1–10:1). The earth is flooded and only Noah's family survives. But Noah gets God's word—a solemn vow—that nothing like that flood will ever happen again. In every case, in every story, God answers human sinfulness with love.

You would think at some point we'd get the message. But the very next story we're told is about the arrogant citizens of Babel who couldn't think of anything more important to do with the great gifts God had given them than to build a monument to themselves (11:1-9). Not surprisingly, their tower topples and they are scattered to the four corners of the earth. Because of their pride and ambition, they are separated by language and custom forever. They are made strangers, uneasy allies at best and warring enemies at worst. Talk about serious consequences! But if we have learned anything from the story up to this point, then we know that right about now God is going to step in. That has been the pattern so far.

A chosen people

And this, finally, brings us to Abraham. "Abraham," God says, "go find Sarah. The two of you need to get busy loading up the wagons. It's time to hit the road."

God is determined to save the world, to bring it back home again. Abraham and Sarah get tapped for the job. God chooses their family—*elects them*. God will bless the whole world through them.

This doesn't really make sense, of course. Abraham and Sarah haven't had any children, and they are too old to start now. Plus, just like the rest of us, Abraham and Sarah are going to mess things up, time and again. In fact, God is going to have to fulfill this plan largely *in spite of* Abraham and Sarah.

But none of this matters. The point is that God is serious about this mission of blessing. And God chooses to do it in partnership with people like Abraham and Sarah—people like us.

The call of Abraham and Sarah is part of the story of a God who answers human sinfulness with unfailing love and a call to mission. How do you see yourself fitting into that story?

The gift is a call

God shows up and promises to bless Abraham and Sarah, granting them safe passage to a new land, where their family will prosper and grow. How do they respond? Well, Abraham's immediate response to this promise is to build an altar and worship God (Genesis 12:7). But the *very next* thing Abraham does, as you have probably guessed, is to act like he never even met God. *Read Genesis 12:10-20,* right now, and see for yourself.

"Sarah?" Abraham calls to his lovely, if elderly, wife. "Honey, we're about to travel through some dangerous territory. The king of this land might get

The gift God gives is always a call. It is a call to witness and to serve, to love and to give ourselves away for the sake of others.

jealous if he sees me with such a beautiful woman. If he does, just do what I tell you. Okay?" Sarah looks at him like he's crazy. But when the time comes, Abraham sends poor Sarah off to serve in the king's harem. Lucky for her, the king catches on and sends her back to her husband. As if *anybody* would want the guy after a stunt like that.

Sarah isn't perfect, either. (Read 18:9-15 sometime.) When the Lord tells her she'll have a baby, all she can do is laugh. Besides, she had already decided God wouldn't keep this promise. In chapter 16, she convinces Abraham to have a child with her servant, Hagar, and claims the boy as her own.

Time and time again, this story will prove that the blessings God promises to Abraham and Sarah really are *gifts* they don't earn or deserve. The truth is, it doesn't seem to matter how clearly God spells out the plan. Abraham and Sarah keep trying to make things happen *their* way. (These two ancient characters are just like us.) And clearly God's blessings are all gift. But those blessings also always come with a *call.* Always.

"Now listen carefully," God said to Abraham. "All of these blessings—this good land, my protection, an influential family—are not for your sake. I am giving these things to you so that, through you, *every* family will be blessed. In fact, these blessings are not yours at all. They are for the sake of the world."

The gift God gives is always a call. It is a call to witness and to serve, to love and to give ourselves away for the sake of others. It is a call to let God use us to make a difference in the world. This was true for Abraham and Sarah. It is true for us too.

How will God's call and blessings impact your life and the way you relate to family, friends, work, community, congregation, nation, those in need, and those who need God?

GROUP TIPS

Your group probably won't have time to read and talk about all of these articles during your time together. That doesn't matter. God is present with you right now, through the Holy Spirit. Encourage group members to read the rest of the articles on their own during the week.

Let the Spirit guide you as you pick one or two articles to focus on right now: "The Gift Is a Call," "A Troubled Family," "And the Point Is...," or "Christmas Stockings." Use the questions at the end of the articles to get your conversation going.

ANOTHER LOOK

If you choose this article, you'll read and discuss another portion of the Bible that sheds light on the main Bible passage.

Have everyone who is willing take turns reading a verse or two at a time from Genesis 12:10-20.

A troubled family

We really are all "family" in a way.

Jews, Christians, and Muslims have a common heritage. We really are all "family" in a way. Abraham is a source of unity between Christians and Jews, but he is honored by Muslims too. Their sacred book, the *Qur'an (ku-RAN)*, describes Abraham as a man of truth and a prophet. And according to Islamic tradition, it was Ishmael, not Isaac, whom Abraham was told to sacrifice (see Genesis 22). Jews trace their ancestry back to Abraham through Isaac, the son of Abraham and Sarah. Muslims trace back to Abraham through Ishmael, the son of Hagar (see Genesis 16). Ishmael and Hagar were kicked out after Isaac was born because Sarah was jealous. But God blessed Ishmael, who also became the father of many descendants.

Read Genesis 21:1-21 for a glimpse into this troubled story.

What kinds of things does a typical family (like yours, for example) fight about? How are larger conflicts around the world similar to the fights families often have? How are they different?

TIP

The names of biblical characters often have special meaning. You may have noticed that Abraham and Sarah are called Abram and Sarai throughout Genesis 11–16. God changed Abram's name to *Abraham* ("father of many nations") and Sarai's name to *Sarah* ("princess"). Their son Isaac's name means "laughter" in Hebrew. (See Genesis 21:6.) What would be more appropriate for a child whose mother laughed at God's promises...and whose father just celebrated his 100th birthday?

And the point is...

Exegesis (*ek-sa-JEE-sis*) is not the name of some awful disease. Actually, it is something you have probably done without thinking about it. Everyone who reads the Bible does it to one extent or another. In fact, exegesis is just a fancy word that describes the act of thinking critically about and interpreting a biblical story or text. And there are different approaches to this. (See page 35.)

This Bible study favors a *narrative* approach, which means paying attention to how a story or text is put together, as a piece of literature. That means, for example, appreciating the way in which

> **The biblical authors have a point they are trying to make. Listen for it.**

each text was crafted by the storytellers and writers and editors (those who put all of these stories together). It means listening for the phrases, words, and images that get repeated along the way. It means looking for the climax in the story, that turning point when the real drama happens. The narrative approach assumes that the person who told this story told it *this way* for a reason.

For example, an *exegete* (and that could mean you) reading the book of Genesis through a narrative lens would notice a pattern like this: people mess up God's creation...they suffer consequences...God steps in to bless them and make things right again...people mess up God's creation...they suffer consequences...God steps in....

An exegete using a narrative approach might also notice that the book of Genesis opens with this pregnant phrase:

In the beginning. Then it describes three key "beginnings" made by God:

1. the beginning of the world (Genesis 1).
2. the beginning of the nations of the world (Genesis 2–11).
3. the beginning of the nation of Israel (Genesis 12–50).

In other words, in the beginning God had a plan. That plan includes the whole world. And, at the center of the plan, is a single nation...a chosen people...a little group of people plucked out of obscurity and blessed beyond all imagination...in order to be a blessing to everyone else.

The stories in the Bible are not *just* stories, of course. God is speaking through them. But they are, in a real way, also *stories*. They are literature. And we can learn a lot from these texts by reading them in that way.

There is something behind the way the biblical storytellers and writers have put these narratives together. The biblical authors have a point they are trying to make.

Listen for it.

How do you usually make sense of the stories you read in the Bible? What do you think about figuring out the point of a biblical story by paying attention to how the story was put together?

christmas stockings

"If three presents were good enough for baby Jesus, that's good enough for us."

That's what my friend, Sam, told me one day. Now, you need to know that Sam was a typical preteen at the time. He was into video games and the kind of music that made his parents' hair stand on end. I'm guessing there was nothing he would have liked better, if truth be told, than to get a whole pile of presents on Christmas morning.

But a couple of years before that, his family had taken an inventory and decided they really didn't *need* anything. They agreed to stop the Christmas shopping madness. Each child in the family would get three presents. That's it: three. Then they would figure out how much money they saved as a result of limiting their Christmas gift shopping and they would use that money to make a difference somewhere. One year they bought a half-ton of socks for homeless shelters in the city. One year they sponsored a needy child halfway around the world.

I'm not sure what Sam would have said if his parents decided they were just kidding and went back to the old gift-giving mayhem on Christmas morning. But I know Christmas in my house was never the same after that. Every single thing we have been given is for the sake of God's world and, especially, for those living on the sharp edge of this life. We are blessed to be a blessing.

"If three presents were good enough for baby Jesus," my son would tell you now, "that's good enough for us."

Indeed.

Name some ways you or your family "bless" others (especially those in need), or ways you could do this.

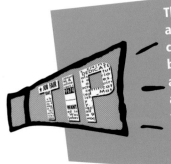

The first five books of the Bible (including Genesis) are part of a special section of the Old Testament called "The Pentateuch" (*pen-ta-TOOCK*). These books include both narrative (stories about God's activity in the world and in the life of the Israelites) and Law (including the Ten Commandments, meant to help people live good and peaceful lives). They help us get to know the God who created us and calls us into partnership.

Wrap up

It is through Jesus that we have the clearest picture of what God is up to. But we see this same God at work here, in the story of Abraham and Sarah. And what we see is a clear pattern emerging. We will see this pattern repeated, again and again, throughout the Bible:

Act 1:   God loves and blesses humanity

Act 2:   Humanity messes up

Act 3:   and suffers the consequences

Act 4:   God answers that mess with unending love and invites the most unlikely people to be the ones to share that love with others.

The next time we're together, we'll look at Exodus 1–2. Here we'll meet more of God's unlikely choices.

What one thing did you learn or hear in this session that will make a difference in your life tomorrow?

End the session with prayer. Do this any way that feels comfortable to your group. You might want to try a "popcorn" prayer. Go around the group and take turns praying a short prayer out loud. This prayer could thank God for something you heard or learned during this session. Or it could ask God for help with something you know you're going to deal with in the coming week. When it comes to you, if you don't feel comfortable praying out loud, pray silently. When you're done, say "Amen!" so the next person knows it is her or his turn.

God's plan is carried out by ordinary people like us.

4 | ON-THE-JOB TRAINING

COME AS YOU ARE

The book of Exodus picks up where Genesis leaves off. Abraham and Sarah are long gone. They died before they could see all of God's promises fulfilled. But God's word is sure. When their grandson Jacob (born to Isaac and Rebekah) moved to Egypt, he took 11 of his sons and their families along with him. (The other son, Joseph, who had an amazingly colorful coat, was already in Egypt.) Just as God had promised, Jacob's family grew there. Life in Egypt was so good for a time that the people seemed to forget the One who blessed them in the first place. And that's when trouble began. Pharaoh (the Egyptian king) and his government, frightened of the growing Hebrew tribe, forced Abraham and Sarah's descendants into slavery and initiated a horrifying plan to reduce the size of the Hebrew population. God's mission to bless the world was in danger. And, once again, God would need people to help get this mission back on track. Some on-the-job training might be needed too.

Spend some time checking in with each other, then take some time to pray. You can do this however you want but, one way or another, begin with prayer asking God to speak to you during this Bible study time. If you want a prayer to pray together out loud, try this one:

O God, you are full of surprises. You have chosen us, of all people. You want to use us to bless the world. Surprise us now, as we meet together to study your Word. Send your Spirit to be here with us. Help us learn from each other and from you. Teach us something that changes us forever. In Jesus' name. Amen

JUST 3 QUESTIONS

Read Exodus 1:1—2:10 out loud. Take turns reading a verse or two at a time. Then spend some time answering these three questions about the reading.

1| What do you think God is doing here?

2| What do you hear God saying to you, personally?

3| What do you hear God saying to us (as a small group, congregation, community, nation)?

Getting the job done

You might have seen at least a clip of the classic movie *The Ten Commandments* (1956, unrated) starring Charlton Heston as Moses. Or you might have met Moses in the film *The Prince of Egypt* (1998, animated, PG). The story of Moses is told here, in the book of Exodus. And you might be surprised to know that, unlike at the movies, Moses is not the star of this story.

As a matter of fact, the starring role is played by God.

Mission possible

As the book of Exodus begins, God's mission to bless the world, through the family of Abraham and Sarah, is in jeopardy. First of all, the people are living in Egypt, instead of in their own land as God had promised. Second, while living in Egypt, their descendants have multiplied (Exodus 1:7). And that made Pharaoh and his government very nervous. Actually, it made them dangerously paranoid. Pharaoh devised a plan to kill any baby boys born to Hebrew mothers (1:15-16). This plan, if successful, would guarantee the elimination of the Hebrew people. And that would mean the end of God's plan.

> God has had a plan, from the beginning of creation, to bring the whole world back home again.

But let's stop the suspense right here: God will win this contest. The Pharaoh might have *looked* like the stronger opponent, especially to the Hebrews, who were commanded to make bricks out of thin air to build his pyramids (5:17-21). This earthly king, however, is no match for the Lord of all creation. Working in mighty ways (see 14:15-31 for the famous "parting of the Red Sea" story) and in quiet ones, God gets the job done. God defeats Pharaoh and leads the people out of slavery, through the wilderness, and toward the promised land. (*Read a summary in 15:1-21*, in the words of the thanksgiving song Moses and his sister, Miriam, sang.)

God has had a plan, from the beginning of creation, to bring the whole world back home again. God has chosen to do this through the family of Abraham and

GROUP TIPS

If your group didn't already do this for "homework," take some time to silently read through the lead article "Getting the Job Done" and talk about it. The questions at the end of the article might help you get your conversation started.

Exodus 15:1-21 is the song the Israelites sang after their escape through the Red Sea. Consider reading it out loud together.

You can also count on this: God calls each one of us to be part of this mission. Bumblers and fumblers. Women and men. Slave and free. Rich and poor. Me. And you.

Sarah. For the sake of all people, of every tribe and every nation, God would not let this chosen people suffer and die.

And the award for best actor in a supporting role goes to...

Are you getting the picture? God heard (2:24). God suffered (2:25). God answered (3:4). God acted (3:8). God entered human history in miraculous ways (3:19-20). God will not let even the most frightened partners (4:13-17) or hardest hearts (5:1-2) stand in the way of this plan. God will be glorified in all the earth (9:29; 19:3-6), among the Hebrews (20:1-3), and even in Pharaoh's Egypt (14:18).

This is God's gig.

But let's be honest. The story wouldn't be the same without Moses. Talk about needing a little on-the-job training! He fumbles and bumbles and stutters his way through this adventure tale. His first effort at dealing with the suffering his people are enduring consists of losing his temper, killing a guy, and fleeing Egypt for his life (2:11-15). When God shows up to tell him his people will be set free, Moses doesn't recognize God (3:13-15); then he argues with God when he finally understands what he's being asked to do (4:1). In fact, Moses argues with God a lot (4:10; 4:13; 5:22-23; etc., etc., etc.). He never does seem sure about whether or not God can be trusted. Moses is an unlikely hero but God uses him to keep the plan going. And because of Moses, we can be confident that God can do something useful...even with people like us.

Moses, though, wouldn't be a part of this story at all if it weren't for a whole bunch of other unlikely people. He survived Pharaoh's plot to kill off

the Hebrew babies only because of a supporting cast that included these amazing women: his selfless mother, his daring sister Miriam (who will also become a leader in the journey out of Egypt and through the wilderness), and Pharaoh's compassionate daughter. And how about those two Hebrew midwives, Shiphrah and Puah? They were midwives because they couldn't have children of their own. And you just couldn't get any lower, in those days, than this: barren, women, and slaves! Yet, they are remembered (*by name*, even though Pharaoh is not!) as heroes in this tale... and God's partners in mission.

You can count on God

God will see this plan fulfilled. God will bless the world and bring it back home again. You can count on it. You can also count on this: God calls each one of us to be part of this mission. Bumblers and fumblers. Women and men. Slave and free. Rich and poor. Me. And you.

How do you see God acting in and through the world today? How is God acting in and through your life?

On the move

Exodus is a Greek word that means "going out." In other words, the story in Exodus is a story about going somewhere. It is about the way people move from one place, one condition, to another.

Take a couple of minutes to *read Exodus 2:11-25*. This *movement*, you'll discover, begins with Moses, who finds himself cast out of his native Egypt and living as "an alien residing in a foreign land" (2:22). But it doesn't stop there.

The Hebrew people *go* from being in bondage to the Egyptian king to serving the Lord. They *go* from building pyramids for Pharaoh to building a tabernacle for God to dwell in (25:1-8).

Moses' older sister Miriam *goes* from being an unnamed girl on the riverbank to being a leader of the people of Israel on their daring escape from Egypt (15:20-21).

Even God moves in this story. God *goes* from being virtually unnoticed even by the descendants of Abraham and Sarah, hidden away up on a mountaintop ("Hey, Moses! Look over here! Yes, right here in this burning bush!" in 3:1-4) to being right in the middle of the people, leading them by a pillar of cloud by day and fire by night (13:21-22).

This story is, in part, about change. Change is what happens to people when God gets involved in their lives.

In what way are you being changed as you become more intentional about following God? What "movement" do you see happening in your life? How do you feel about that?

GROUP TIPS

Pick one or two articles to talk about: "On the Move," "Let My People Go," "Back to the Sources?," or "No Holding Back." Be sure to invite input from those group members who haven't had a chance to choose an article in previous meetings. Use the questions at the end of the articles to get your conversation going.

Encourage group members to read the rest of articles on their own during the week.

ANOTHER LOOK

If you choose this article, you'll read and discuss another portion of the Bible that sheds light on the main Bible passage.

Have everyone who is willing take turns reading a verse or two at a time from Exodus 2:11-25.

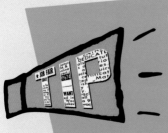

Biblical scholars identify the story of the exodus (the story of how God brought the people out of Egypt) as THE event the rest of the Bible looks to in order to make sense of things. This is because, in so many ways, God's people discover who they really are in this story.

Let my people go

There are few stories that have captured the imagination of people in trouble more than this one. *Read Exodus 3:1-12* right now to get an even better sense of where this story is going.

The Hebrew people were living in bondage, enslaved to a merciless king. Suddenly, up on a mountainside, God appears, which makes even the ground beneath Moses' feet holy. The lowly shepherd becomes a hero. And every good thing ever dreamed of seems somehow within reach.

"I have heard your cries," the Lord declares. "And I will rescue you. Count on it."

Is it any wonder, for example, that this story gave comfort and hope to African Americans, living in slavery in the United States? Or that oppressed people around the globe today look to the God of this story for liberation?

Make no mistake: Freedom from slavery did not mean "anything goes" for the people. They were freed from bondage to Pharaoh in order to love and serve the Lord (19:8). That's how it's supposed to work. And when it didn't, the people found themselves in need of God's mercy and forgiveness. (The story of the most infamous calf

ever sculpted is told in chapter 32). But freedom, in Exodus, is more than just freedom from sin. The Exodus event suggests that God is interested in even more than that.

In the Exodus story we meet a God who opposes the institutionalized forces of evil, the demons of economic and political tyranny, and the horrors of slavery. This God stands with people who are oppressed, outcast, or poor; suffers with them; works on their behalf to bring justice and peace; and stops at nothing to set them free.

This God cares about people on the edges...and wants our help in making things right for them.

> God's agenda includes setting people free from tyranny, injustice, and poverty. And if that is God's agenda, it must be our agenda too. What do you think about that?

This God cares about people on the edges...and wants our help in making things right for them.

Biblical scholars identify the story of the exodus (the story of how God brought the people out of Egypt) as THE event the rest of the Bible looks to in order to make sense of things. This is because, in so many ways, God's people discover who they really are in this story. The prophets refer to it (Isaiah 11:15-16; Micah 6:2-4). The psalmist sings about it (Psalms 77; 106, for example). And the Gospel writers tell about Moses showing up one day to talk with Jesus (Matthew 17:1-3; Mark 9:2-4; Luke 9:28-31).

Back to the sources?

Most scholars don't spend a lot of time worrying about whether or not the exodus from Egypt "really happened." There is some archaeological evidence that there were slaves, possibly Hebrew, in Egypt in the late Bronze Age (1500-1000 B.C.). But there is no real historical record of it in Egypt. The biblical story itself doesn't help much. Notice: no dates are given. No Pharaohs are named. It's as if history didn't really matter much to people who first told—and heard—this story. They had something else on their minds.

Scholars who have studied the text, which doesn't always flow very smoothly, have come to believe that the stories of several tribes were brought together over time to form, not only Exodus, but the first five books of the Old Testament. Each of these tribes, or sources, had its own stories...and its own agendas. Each lived in a different context, asked different questions, came at things from a different perspective. And each had something important to say about God.

> **When God makes a promise, you can count on it.**

Bringing it all together

At some point, someone wove all these stories together to give us the book of Exodus in its final form. Many scholars agree that this probably happened during an especially horrific period in the history of Israel. Between about 700-400 B.C., the people of Israel experienced one awful catastrophe after another: war, defeat, poverty, exile. God seemed very far away. The story of the exodus from Egypt gave them hope. Here was a picture of a God who wins the day for the chosen people, even when the odds are stacked high against them and all seems lost.

In the midst of such trouble, getting all of the "history" right was the last thing on anybody's mind. And frankly, there is just no way for us to piece it together after all these years. Besides, there is this very important point to make: *God's plan will not be foiled by any earthly power. God's mission will be fulfilled!*

When God makes a promise, you can count on it.

This is a message that people over the centuries have needed to hear. We still do.

How important is it for you to know exactly who wrote the stories in the Bible and when and why? Does the story of the exodus mean something to you even without this information?

GROUP TIPS

RIGHT TO THE POINT

If you choose this article, you'll focus on one key thing about God and following Jesus.

Take turns reading Exodus 3:1-12.

BIBLE BASICS

If you choose this article, you'll learn more about the Bible and listening for what God is saying through these words.

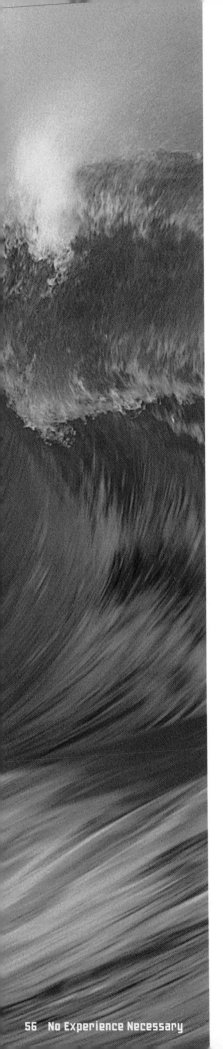

No holding back

Being God's partner in mission does not guarantee an easy path through life. The book of Psalms is full of songs like this one, hoping against hope for an answer from a God who seems very far away.

I call out to God without holding back. Oh, that God would listen to me! When I was in deep trouble, I searched for the Lord. All night long I pray, with hands lifted toward heaven, pleading. There can be no joy for me until he acts. I think of God, and I moan, overwhelmed with longing for his help.

You don't let me sleep. I am too distressed even to pray! I think of the good old days, long since ended, when my nights were filled with joyful songs. I search my soul and think about the difference now. Has the Lord rejected me forever? Will he never again show me favor? Is his unfailing love gone forever? Have his promises permanently failed? Has God forgotten to be kind? Has he slammed the door on his compassion?

And I said, "This is my fate, that the blessings of the Most High have changed to hatred." I recall all you have done, O Lord; I remember your wonderful deeds of long ago. They are constantly in my thoughts. I cannot stop thinking about them. O God, your ways are holy. Is there any god as mighty as you? You are the God of miracles and wonders!

Being God's partner in mission does not guarantee an easy path through life.

You demonstrate your awesome power among the nations. You have redeemed your people by your strength, the descendants of Jacob and of Joseph by your might.

When the Red Sea saw you, O God, its waters looked and trembled! The sea quaked to its very depths. The clouds poured down their rain; the thunder rolled and crackled in the sky. Your arrows of lightning flashed. Your thunder roared from the whirlwind; the lightning lit up the world! The earth trembled and shook. Your road led through the sea, your pathway through the mighty waters—a pathway no one knew was there! You led your people along that road like a flock of sheep, with Moses and Aaron as their shepherds. (Psalm 77 New Living Translation)

Do you know what it's like to feel like the writer of this psalm? What got the writer through those hard times? What gets you through?

Wrap up

G od, not Moses or Miriam, is the star of this story. But they, and others like them, played an important role in God's plan to bless the world. So do we.

We are leaving the five books of the Pentateuch for now. (We'll come back to them in future units.) Next time, we'll be diving into 1 Samuel, beginning in chapter 8. This will mean jumping ahead a few generations: When we pick up the story, Moses will have been long gone. Although Moses never lived to see all of God's promises fulfilled, God has been faithful. The people of Israel have settled in their new land. And they have become a great nation. Now they say they want a king. Apparently, they have forgotten that they already have one.

This should be interesting.

What one thing did you learn or hear in this session that will make a difference in your life tomorrow?

End the session with prayer. If you didn't try a "popcorn" prayer last time, consider trying it now. If you did try it and it worked, do it again!

GROUP TIPS

RIGHT HERE, RIGHT NOW

If you choose this article, you'll read about real people becoming involved in God's mission to bless and save the world.

GET GOING

Read "Wrap Up" out loud or silently. Then go around the group and quickly answer the question at the end.

Make sure everyone knows where and when your small group is meeting next. Then talk about whether your group wants to do any "homework." Do you want to agree to try to read the next session—or part of the session (like the lead article)—ahead of time?

Sometimes God has to carry out the plan *in spite of* us.

5 | a HUMAN RESOURCE PROBLEM

COME AS YOU ARE

Through Jesus, we have been able to catch a glimpse of who God is, what God is up to, and how God goes about doing it. We know that God is on a mission to bless and save the whole world. And as we've worked our way through the Old Testament, we have seen this pattern form:

Act 1: God loves, blesses, creates.

Act 2: People try to go their own way instead of following God.

Act 3: They end up in a big mess that threatens not only their own happiness but also God's plan.

Act 4: Then at just the right time, God steps in to save them and invites them (again and again!) to be a part of the plan to bring the whole world back home.

As we pick up the story in 1 Samuel 8, we are right at the beginning of yet another "Act 2." God has blessed Israel through the leadership of the prophet, Samuel. Even Israel's enemies have seen these blessings and given glory to God! But the people are restless. And they are just about to mess everything up. Again.

Spend some time checking in with each other, then take some time to pray. You can do this however you want but, one way or another, begin with prayer asking God to speak to you during this Bible study time. If you want a prayer to pray together out loud, try this one:

Mighty and merciful God, thank you for calling us to be a part of your plan in the world. And thank you for being gentle with us when we are slow to answer. Send your Spirit to be with us as we hear from each other and from you. Bless our study. Be in our conversation. Help us grow so you can use us to make a difference in the world. In Jesus' name. Amen

JUST 3 QUESTIONS

Read 1 Samuel 8 out loud. Take turns reading a verse or two at a time. Then spend some time answering these three questions about the reading.

1 | **What do you think God is doing here?**

2 | **What do you hear God saying to you, personally?**

3 | **What do you hear God saying to us (as a small group, congregation, community, nation)?**

GROUP TIPS

COME AS YOU ARE

Take this time to catch up with each other. If you want a starting point for your conversation, try this: "Tell about something you found particularly meaningful or challenging in last week's articles or group discussion."

JUST 3 QUESTIONS

Has your group been skipping one of the three questions because you don't have enough time? Or have you avoided one of the questions for some other reason? Try answering THAT question first this time. Expect God to speak to you in new and surprising ways.

Facing Challenges

GROUP TIPS

HEART OF THE MATTER

If your group didn't already do this for "homework," take some time to silently read the lead article, "Facing Challenges." Then take a few minutes to talk about it. The questions at the end of the article might help you get your conversation started.

A lot has happened since we left Moses, Miriam, and the Israelites in the wilderness. After the big escape from Egypt, God gave them Ten Commandments (Exodus 20) and a bunch of other laws to help them live well. In fact, there was no aspect of their lives that God didn't address. There were laws about how to worship, work, treat both family members and strangers, marry and bury and eat and disagree with each other. The people couldn't exactly keep all these laws, of course. Nobody could. And many of these laws don't make sense outside of that particular day and age. But having such an exhaustive list of them makes it clear that God wants to be right at the center of our lives. (Look at Exodus 20–Deuteronomy 34 for the whole long list of laws.)

> God wants to be right at the center of our lives.

The people lived in that wilderness for 40 years. Moses himself never made it out. He died there, trusting that God's promises would be fulfilled. And then finally, led by Moses' assistant, Joshua, the people made their way into the promised land. They settled down, built homes, planted crops, and grew strong (see Joshua 1–24 for more).

For generations after Joshua died, this new nation was ruled by women and men called judges. Many of these judges were faithful to God. Some were not. All along they were surrounded by enemies and often under attack. The memory of God's salvation and the great exodus from Egypt grew dim (Judges 1–21). The God who wanted to be right at the center of everything became less and less important in the lives of the people God had chosen.

Foolishly, the people turned away from God to their enemies' gods, believing this would give them added protection. It didn't. Without the Lord as their ruler and king, "the people did what was right in their own eyes" (Judges 21:25). They seemed destined for disaster.

And so did God's plan.

God was right, of course. The whole king idea ended up being a mixed bag.

God intervenes

That's when God stepped in. In a characteristically unexpected way, God chose a lowly woman named Hannah to bring a new prophet to Israel. His name was Samuel. He led the nation in a return to the Lord. They got rid of their idols and peace once again came to their land (see 1 Samuel 1–7 for more).

Things were so good, in fact, that even their enemies could see what the Lord had done in Israel. Other nations knew the old story about the miraculous escape from Egypt. They had been out-fought and overwhelmed by this God in battle. Even their priests, serving at the altar of idols, told them to "give glory to the God of Israel" (1 Samuel 6:5)!

In so many ways, God's plan to bless the world through the people of Israel, and to finally really be the Lord of all creation, appeared to be working.

People mess it up

As Samuel grew old, however, the people of Israel worried. Samuel's sons didn't seem likely candidates to replace their dad. Forgetting God's promise of blessing, the people asked for the one thing they thought would protect them: a "real" king. Apparently, they had forgotten they already had one. Samuel got angry at the people's request and God wasn't too happy, either.

"It's not you they're rejecting, Samuel," God said. "They are rejecting me. Mark my words, they will regret this. But if it's a *real* king they want, fine. Give it to them."

God was right, of course. The whole king idea ended up being a mixed bag. The first one, Saul, turned power crazy. He got himself and his son killed, and almost destroyed the nation (1 Samuel 9–2 Samuel 2). Even Israel's greatest king,

David, turned in a less than stellar performance, along the way committing betrayal, adultery, and murder (2 Samuel).

It seems more clear than ever that if God is serious about having people like us as partners in mission, it is going to mean getting things done almost *in spite of* us.

God's plan to partner with people to bless the world seems to hit one snag after another but God is patient with us. How was this good news for the people of Israel? How is it good news for you...and for the church today?

Getting the story straight

There are important stories in the Bible about women who have been God's partners in mission—but it would be easy to miss them. The way the story has traditionally been told, in sermons and Bible studies and even at the movies, women have had supporting roles at best.

Missing in action?

Women are "missing" from the story we've been told partly because of the culture we live in. And we see evidence of women being undervalued in the biblical stories themselves. Remember Abraham's willingness to sacrifice Sarah to save his own skin (Session 3)? Even more horrifying, Abraham's nephew, Lot, risked the honor and lives of his own daughters to protect some men he had just met (Genesis 19:1-8). You might have noticed, too, that women are hardly ever mentioned in genealogies, as if only the men in a family tree mattered.

But that is not what God intends. Women do matter to God. In fact, in completely countercultural fashion, God consistently put women at the center of this unfolding drama.

At the center

Think back for a minute to Genesis. Sarah, and not just Abraham, was called to be God's partner in this mission to bless the world (Genesis 17:15-19).

The story of Moses' courageous older sister, who helped save the day in Exodus 2, is another example of a woman at the center of the action. Miriam helped lead the people through the Red Sea (Exodus 15). She and brother Aaron helped hold Moses accountable for questionable decisions (Numbers 12:1) though they whined because he always got all the credit (Numbers 12:2) and Miriam suffered consequences for this. She is one of the few people in the Bible to whom God spoke directly (Numbers 12:5) and she is the only woman remembered as a descendant of Levi, one of Jacob's 12 sons (1 Chronicles 6:3).

And here, in 1 Samuel, the story opens up with God's plan in jeopardy. The people of Israel have wandered far away from God and lost track of the mission. They need new direction and a new leader. So what does God do? Something countercultural, of course. Hannah is chosen to be God's partner in getting the plan back on track. *Read 1 Samuel 1* right now to see it for yourself.

In spite of it all

There is no getting around the fact that life was hard for women in biblical times. Tragically, in some parts of the world it isn't any better today. The fact that women are often still "missing in action" in sermons and Bible studies suggests there is still a long way to go even here at home. But for God, women matter. In spite of harsh cultural realities, women have always been at the center of the action in God's mission to bless the world.

They still are.

God didn't follow the established order in biblical times. How could you be a partner with God, making change happen for the sake of a better world?

GROUP TIPS

Pick one or two articles to talk about: "Getting the Story Straight," "Told You So," "Piecing the Story Together," or "The Photograph." Use the questions at the end of the articles to get your conversation going.

Don't be frustrated because you're not getting through every article during your time together. Just encourage group members to read the rest of the articles on their own during the week.

ANOTHER LOOK

If you choose this article, you'll read and discuss another portion of the Bible that sheds light on the main Bible passage.

Have everyone who is willing take turns reading a verse or two at a time from 1 Samuel 1.

Told you so

Israel's first king was named Saul. He was followed by David, definitely a better pick, and David's son, Solomon. David and Solomon weren't so bad (as kings go) but, as God warned and Samuel predicted, having a "real" king never really did protect the people from hardship or war. Partly, this was because the people too often allowed their kings to inherit the position, rather than prayerfully seeking out God's direction each time about who the best person was for the job. Partly, it was because even the best kings ended up, like Saul, thinking they were all that (which means they became too big for their britches). *Read 1 Samuel 14:24-30* for a taste of what life was like under such a king. Mostly, it was because the people of Israel

THE OLD TESTAMENT WORLD

seemed to totally forget that they were called to be partners with God in blessing the world. They were only worried about saving their own skin.

What were they thinking?

In the end, they had a series of rotten kings who made bad alliances with enemy nations rather than trusting in and following God. The whole sorry story, stretching over a dozen or so generations, is told in the books of 1 and 2 Samuel, 1 and 2 Kings, and 1 and 2 Chronicles. After hundreds of years of this sort of nonsense, the nation that once had so much promise was in a big mess.

First, it split into two kingdoms (north and south) by its own internal politics, following the death of King Solomon. Then it fell to its enemies. The Northern Kingdom (called Israel) was defeated by the Assyrians in the 700s B.C. The Southern Kingdom (called Judah) fell to the Babylonians in 587 B.C. The cities were devastated. The lands were overrun. The temple, at the center of Jerusalem, was leveled. The people were hauled off into exile, forced to serve foreign kings and worship other gods.

"Told you so," Samuel might have said, had he still been around when all these events came to pass. But he was long gone by then.

Thinking about all the dumb decisions God's people made back then, and how often they seemed to forget who they were, it would be easy to ask, "What were they *thinking*?!?"

But then again, they could probably ask the same thing of us.

What things distract us, as individuals and as the church, from the mission to which God has called us today?

The nation that once had so much promise was in a big mess.

Piecing the story together

Okay, this probably sounds silly to say but it's important to remember: The Old Testament is *old*. It is so old, in fact, that all of the "original" manuscripts have long ago disappeared. Disintegrated, even. What we have today are *copies* of the originals.

Now some of these copies are incredibly old, themselves. The Old Testament manuscripts we have are considered, by historians and archeologists, to be exceptionally reliable.

But that doesn't mean there aren't difficulties in working with them. And the books of Samuel are among the most challenging.

A few ancient copies of Samuel have actually been found. But many of the oldest are in poor condition. Some of them contain what we are pretty sure are scribal errors (things that were copied down incorrectly) and questionable translations. There was a lot of controversy among biblical scholars during the nineteenth and twentieth centuries over which of the ancient Samuel texts should be considered authoritative. In other words, if two ancient manuscripts disagree, which one do we believe?

The situation was somewhat improved, beginning in the late 1940s, with the discovery of the Dead Sea Scrolls in Qumran. A copy of Samuel found there is estimated to be older than any other Samuel manuscript ever found...by about 1,000 years.

Today, biblical scholars are relying on more than 10 ancient copies of Samuel, originally written in multiple languages (including Syriac, Old Latin, Greek, and Palestinian). They check and cross-check their work against all of these old manuscripts in order to produce the best English translations possible.

What is your reaction to all this information about the history of the biblical texts? Why do you react that way?

GROUP TIPS

RIGHT TO THE POINT

If you choose this article, you'll focus on one key thing about God and following Jesus.

Take turns reading 1 Samuel 14:24-30.

BIBLE BASICS

If you choose this article, you'll learn more about the Bible and listening for what God is saying through these words.

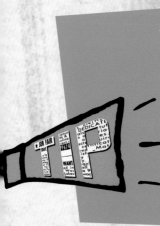

Whether or not God was in favor of giving Israel a king, once it happened, the issue quickly became: What *kind* of king should Israel have? The answer: Israel didn't need a king to lead it into battle but a king who had been anointed by God. (To be anointed is to receive a blessing, along with oil poured on your head, because God has chosen you for a special task.) When Jesus showed up announcing "the kingdom of God," his followers would come to see Jesus as the Anointed One, the King they had been waiting for. In fact, the Hebrew word for *anointed one* is "messiah." In Greek, the word is *christos*, or Christ. Both of these titles would be used for Jesus.

The photograph

The only explanation for how I got here... from there...is God.

She was feeling a little nervous as she stood waiting for him in his office. The office wasn't much to look at, pretty ragged, in fact. But she knew that what lay beneath the humble appearance was a very, very rich man. He had a reputation in the community for being smart at business...and a little ruthless. But he also was known as a man who gave a lot away. A school was named after him, for goodness' sake. And she had a church to build.

Her congregation had struggled to turn things around after decades of decline. They had worked hard to be welcoming and inviting. They had changed everything, in fact, in order to reach a new generation, who spoke a new language, in the middle of a changing community. But one thing hadn't changed. They didn't have a lot of money. And they needed it if they were going to build the community center they believed the kids in the neighborhood needed.

She was looking at an old photograph on the wall when he came in. It was black and white, taken around 1940 or so, she guessed. In the background was a little house in terrible disrepair. Obviously a very poor family lived there, she thought. Standing in front of it was a 10-year-old boy, in the most raggedy clothes you can imagine.

"That's me," he said in a low voice. "And that's the house I grew up in."

"You must feel very proud," she said, turning around to meet him. "You've come far."

"No," he answered. "Not proud at all. I feel thankful. The only explanation for how I got here...from there...is God."

He took the picture off the wall, turned it over, and handed it to her. Written on the back were these words: "1 Corinthians 1:26-31."

She left his office that day with a down payment for a new community center. And she'd be the first one to tell you: She wasn't feeling proud about what she had accomplished.

She was thankful.

In what way has God accomplished great things in your life almost *in spite of* you? For what are you most thankful?

Many scholars believe that Samuel was originally one book named "Samuel" because it began with the story of this famous prophet. But when it was translated from the original Hebrew into Greek and Latin, it was written (as was the custom then) on papyrus scrolls. It was too long for one scroll so it was split up into two books or scrolls: 1 and 2 Samuel. Oddly enough, this decision meant Samuel doesn't even appear in the second book that bears his name!

Wrap up

God has a plan to partner with people to bless the whole world. This plan is as old as time. But, just like the people of Israel in Samuel's day, we keep messing it up. God is infinitely patient, loves us no matter what, and is determined to fulfill this plan even in spite of us! But that doesn't mean there aren't serious consequences for our stubborn, shortsighted (even stupid!) behavior. Next time, we'll read Isaiah 1:1—2:5 and see the mess the people of Israel got themselves into when they turned away from God...and we'll look at the God who stays faithful to them anyway.

Where (in what place, situation, or relationship) do you think God might be calling you to make a difference this week?

Pray together in any way that seems right for your group. But be sure to pray out loud. Since you've been meeting together for awhile now, if you haven't already done this, try having everyone take a turn praying. Use the "popcorn" prayer method, if you haven't tried it yet. If you have, go a little further. Go around the circle, giving each person a chance. But take your time. Pray about the things that are on your heart. Pray for your group, your congregation, the church in the world. Pray for everyone out there who is hungry today...and everyone out there who is hungry for God. Don't worry about saying the right words or sounding holy or inspiring anybody. Let the words just come, knowing that God is listening...and loving you.

RIGHT HERE, RIGHT NOW

If you choose this article, you'll read about real people becoming involved in God's mission to bless and save the world.

GET GOING

Read "Wrap Up" out loud or silently. Then go around the group and quickly answer the question at the end of the reading.

If group members haven't already read chapter 2 in the book *No Experience Necessary: Everybody's Welcome*, consider doing that this week.

It's time to start thinking about what you're going to do next. Some people in your group may want to continue meeting for Bible study because the experience has been a blessing to them. If that's the case, consider how your group can be a blessing to others. One idea: Those who want to continue doing Bible study could split up into two groups for the next unit. That way each person can invite a friend to come. (This idea might produce mixed feelings in your group. Talk about it, anyway.)

6 | CONTRACT RENEWAL

COME AS YOU ARE

Samuel cautioned the people that giving their loyalty to any king besides God would end in disaster—and he was right. Generations after Samuel's warning, another prophet looks out over the devastated countryside. God has not given up on the plan to bless the world through these people. But they have rebelled against God and this plan. Even the heavens and the earth testify against them. They have ignored the needy in their midst. They have lived greedily, without regard for others and without thanks to God. They have wanted to be like other nations. Their worship lives have become routine and meaningless.

The prophet Isaiah's job isn't to predict the future (and we shouldn't try to use these words for that purpose, either). Isaiah's job is to help his people remember who they are. He does that, not so much with storytelling, but with a kind of poetry. These words sound strange to our ears today. But the message is as meaningful as ever.

Spend some time checking in with each other, then take some time to pray. As always, how you do this is up to you. Hopefully, you have become more comfortable praying out loud together. Maybe you are even taking turns praying out loud. In your opening prayer, be sure to invite the Spirit to open your hearts and minds to each other and to God's voice. If it still seems helpful to pray a prayer together out loud, use this prayer:

Faithful God, thank you for bringing us together again. Thank you for all of the good changes that are happening in our lives because of what we are learning in this small group. Thank you for loving us and calling us to be a part of what you are up to in the world. Thank you for sending your Spirit to be here with us now. Bless our conversation. Open our hearts and minds to each other and to you. In Jesus' name. Amen

JUST 3 QUESTIONS

Read Isaiah 1:1–2:5 out loud. Take turns reading a verse or two at a time. Then spend some time answering these three questions about the reading.

1 | What do you think God is doing here?

2 | What do you hear God saying to you, personally?

3 | What do you hear God saying to us (as a small group, congregation, community, nation)?

For this session have markers and a white board or large sheet of chart paper available for "Another Look."

COME AS YOU ARE

Check in with each other for a few minutes. If you want a starting point for your conversation, try this: "As you get close to the end of this unit, what ideas are beginning to shape or reshape the way you think about God, the world, the Bible, your congregation, or your life?"

If the group has read chapter 2 in *No Experience Necessary: Everybody's Welcome*, take a few minutes to discuss reactions to the book.

JUST 3 QUESTIONS

Sometimes one person in the group will have a question or a concern that could take up the whole discussion time. Once in a while, because of extraordinary circumstances, the group will want and need to spend the whole time listening to and supporting that person. But no one person should dominate the group's agenda every time. If that is happening, gently tell that person that others need a chance to talk too.

Promises you can count on

E ven if you're not familiar with the Old Testament book, you may have already heard a lot of passages from Isaiah. That's largely because the Revised Common Lectionary (a list many congregations use to decide which Bible readings to use in worship each week) includes more passages from Isaiah than any other Old Testament book, especially during Advent, Christmas, Lent, and Holy Week.

> **Jesus was the one they had been waiting for all along.**

Isaiah has been an important book to Christians since the very beginning. In fact, remember when Jesus showed up at the temple in Nazareth as a young preacher ready to begin his public ministry (Session 1), he read from the book of the prophet Isaiah:

"The Spirit of the Lord is upon me, because he has anointed me to bring good news to the poor. He has sent me to proclaim release to the captives and recovery of sight to the blind, to let the oppressed go free, to proclaim the year of the Lord's favor" (Luke 4:18-19).

Compare this with Isaiah 61:1-2.

A promise kept

These words from Isaiah had given hope to Jesus' ancestors in Israel throughout centuries of war, exile, scarcity, and fear. They believed one day God would send a Messiah, an "anointed" one, a savior who would make everything right again.

After Jesus read these words, he put the book down (actually, it was a scroll) and announced, "Well, you're looking at the real deal, folks." As you might remember from Session 1, the people got mad, thinking Jesus was making fun of them, and tried to throw him over a cliff. But we know now that there was nothing funny about it. Jesus was serious. God's promises are too.

After his death, Jesus' followers went back and read that passage and others like it from Isaiah. Isaiah helped them make sense of what happened to Jesus and why. Isaiah helped them see Jesus for who he really was. Jesus was the one they had been waiting for all along.

GROUP TIPS

HEART OF THE MATTER

If necessary, take some time to silently read through the lead article "Promises You Can Count On." Then take a few minutes to talk about it. The questions at the end of the article might help you get your conversation started.

Have someone read Isaiah 61:1-2 out loud and compare it to Luke 4:18-19 (printed in the article).

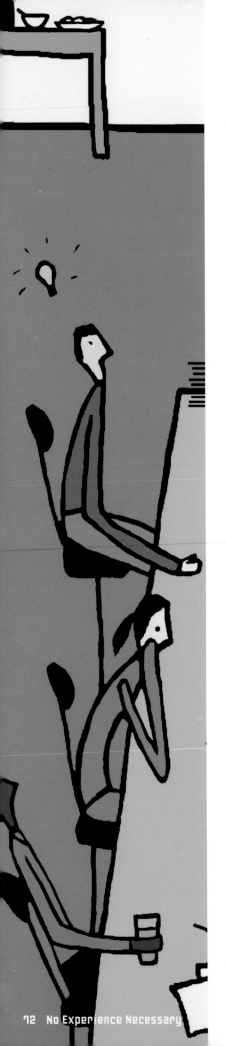

One way or another, through the people God has called to be partners in mission, the world will come to worship the one who created it and loves it. God's kingdom will come.

A timeless message

Isaiah's main job, however, didn't actually have anything to do with Jesus. Seven hundred years before Jesus was even born (and for centuries after that), during the most awful times in their history, this book helped God's people see *themselves* more clearly.

Picture this: It is about 700 B.C. Samuel is long gone. Israel's greatest kings, David and Solomon, have long since passed away. Their descendants have done a so-so job of ruling and many of them have been outright failures. They find themselves now under attack. The Assyrian army has ravaged their countryside. An army stands outside the gates of Jerusalem. All hope seems lost. Just then, a voice from God rings out: "Hear, O heavens, and listen, O earth!" Isaiah shouts. "For the LORD has spoken" (Isaiah 1:2)!

The message the prophet Isaiah delivered in that terrible day held the people accountable for the mess they had gotten themselves into. But it gave them hope too.

First, Isaiah said, *you can count on God's promises*. God promised to bless the descendants of Abraham and Sarah. This promise can't ever be taken away, no matter what. Even at their worst, these people were called "children" of God (1:2). Again and again, regardless of how disobedient (and, sometimes, just plain dumb) the people have been, God renews their contract.

Second, just because God's promises are forever doesn't mean they can be taken for granted. *God's blessings come with a responsibility to bless others*, especially the poor, the oppressed, and the weak (1:16-17). The people of Isaiah's time weren't doing their job. And that

meant serious consequences, not only for them but for all creation (1:2).

But finally, Isaiah said, *God will have the last word*. God's mission to bring the whole world back home again will be fulfilled (2:1-5). All the nations will one day see God's power. They may see it as God's people suffer the consequences of failing to answer their call. Or they may see it as God's people prosper because they are doing what the Lord has asked of them. But they will see it. One way or another, through the people God has called to be partners in mission, the world will come to worship the one who created it and loves it. God's kingdom will come.

That is a promise worth hanging onto.

Isaiah says that the key to a good life is answering the call to be part of God's mission and that trouble happens when we don't. Have you seen this played out in your own life? In your congregation?

A really big deal

The idea that we are "saved by grace through faith" is a big deal for a lot of Christians. We got it from the apostle Paul, mostly, who wrote about salvation in his letters (see Romans 5, for example). His concern was primarily about *how* we get saved. And he wanted us to know that our salvation is a gift from God, not something we can earn. In fact, he used Abraham and Sarah as an example of how it all works (see Romans 4).

But what is salvation, anyway? Typically, people tend to define *salvation* as something like "forgiveness of sins" or "going to heaven." But salvation is a lot more than that. Salvation is also about the here and now. And Isaiah helps us see it. In fact, Isaiah talks about salvation more than any other book in the Old Testament.

Across all 66 chapters, the book of Isaiah describes the "salvation" of God, often calling God "savior" and promising that God will "save" the people of Israel and the whole world. The words *salvation* and *savior* don't show up at all in any of the other Old Testament prophetic books (except a handful of times in Jeremiah), but Isaiah uses them dozens of times. *Read the following passages in Isaiah and make a list of all the images Isaiah uses to talk about God's saving activity: 25:6-9; 43:10-12; 60:18-21; 62:1-4.*

Here and now

When God saves us, Isaiah tells us, we are given a new name, a new home, and a new life. We are rescued from violence, hunger, pain, death, humiliation, and fear. We are given a new relationship with God and a new job. We become witnesses to what God is doing in the world! And, through us, all people will be gathered to God.

The gift of salvation is a much bigger deal than just having our sins forgiven. It changes everything. And it is most definitely NOT something we can keep to ourselves.

> **The gift of salvation is a much bigger deal than just having our sins forgiven. It changes everything.**

According to Isaiah, how is the gift of salvation connected to a call to be a part of God's mission in the world?

The only thing that matters is God's message.

Just a messenger

Unlike the books of Jeremiah and Ezekiel, two of the other well-known prophets in the Old Testament, the book of Isaiah does not begin by telling the story of the prophet's call to ministry. It's almost like we're being told, "Look, I'm not what's important here. The only thing that matters is God's message." Not a bad thing for all of us to remember.

But the story of Isaiah's call does show up eventually, in chapter 6. *Read Isaiah 6:1-8* now. Notice how Isaiah's initial reaction to meeting God is an awareness of his own inadequacy and sinfulness. "Woe is me!" he cried. "I am lost!" Notice, too, that before Isaiah could even ask for it to be done, God had "blotted out" his sin and taken it away (6:7).

When God calls, "Whom shall I send?" (6:8) and looks at us, it isn't because we have earned it. Isaiah didn't. Standing in the presence of the holy God, he knew it too. God's call is a gift. That's why forgiveness comes along with it.

"Here I am, send me!" can only slip through the lips of those who know they don't deserve it.

Can you think of a time when you heard God calling you to do something and you responded by doing it, even if it was hard or scary?

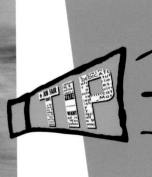

The Hebrew word *nabi*, which means "one who is called" or "one who is called upon," is most often used for *prophet*. Biblical prophets, like Isaiah, didn't predict the future, and we shouldn't try to use their words for that purpose today. Rather, a prophet is one through whom God speaks about why things are happening right now and/or why they have happened in the past. The prophets helped people see God at work in their lives and in the world, and called them to faithfully follow this righteous and powerful God.

A long history

At the heart of Isaiah is a message of hope in the midst of really dark days and a call to faithfulness so powerful that people of each new generation are tempted to read this book as though it was written especially for them. For this reason, the book of Isaiah has a very long history of interpretation.

For each generation

Scholars agree a prophet named Isaiah was at work in Jerusalem around the time of the Assyrian attack in 701 B.C. He told his people that their troubles were directly related to the fact that they

> **Through the words of Isaiah, each new generation hears God's voice speaking to it, about what has been and what is to come.**

had rebelled against God and refused to participate in God's mission, as seen in the way they treated the outcast and marginalized. The consequences were tragic. This is the basic story of the book of Isaiah, and it belongs to this prophet from the eighth century B.C.

But within the text itself there is some evidence that others, who recognized themselves and their situation in Isaiah's words, added to this book over hundreds of years. A significant addition or revision of the book occurred when Jerusalem finally fell to the Babylonians in 587 B.C. Suddenly, as Jerusalem lay in ruins, Isaiah's words made more sense than ever.

Through the words of Isaiah, each new generation hears God's voice speaking to it, about what has been and what is to come.

The point of the story

For much of the nineteenth and twentieth centuries, scholars worked to sort out the detailed history of Isaiah. For a long time, they tried to say that Isaiah could be divided into three distinct sections (chapters 1–39; 40–55; 56–66), each written at a different time by a different author. But in recent years, scholars have become less certain about this theory. The fact is, at some point, someone took all of the stories connected to the book of Isaiah and shaped them into a single story. And this story has a point.

Contemporary biblical scholars don't all describe the meaning of Isaiah in the same way. Some say Isaiah is a call to put our trust in God rather than foreign powers or military might. Others would argue that Isaiah is a call to trust God in every aspect of our lives. But everyone agrees that Isaiah includes a word of promise (nothing can ever separate us from God, who loves us and calls us into partnership) and a word of judgment (there will be trouble when we fail to answer that call).

And no one doubts that God has something important to say to us, right now, through the book of Isaiah.

The words of Isaiah held people accountable for the way they treated the poor, outcast, and marginalized. What do you think God would hold us accountable for today?

The long and short of it

I was driving along I-90, heading north toward Wisconsin, when I spotted this license plate:

Now, I thought, getting one new beginning would be awesome enough, but to be given a second one? To know, in fact, that there is no limit to the number of new beginnings God is willing to give us?

How cool is that?

Think for a minute about some "new beginning" God has given to you. How has your response honored God? How have you used your "blessing" to be a blessing to others?

On the surface, the book of Isaiah seems to be almost entirely concerned with the fate of Israel and the people of Jerusalem. But, in fact, God's purposes extend to the whole world. We know this because of Jesus. But it is also clear in the text of Isaiah itself. Isaiah 2:1-5 is a key passage for understanding God's purposes. It describes God's vision for the world, the reality God is working to create, and the focal point of God's mission—and ours! In other words, one way to talk about what God is up to is to say simply this: *God is working to make Isaiah 2:1-5 a reality.*

Wrap up

The book of Isaiah has a long history. It has been a reminder of God's promises to people in terrible circumstances. It has been a word of judgment to people who have rebelled against God and forgotten who they are. Each new generation has looked back to Isaiah in order to make sense of the present. And there, in the prophet's words, each generation has found hope for the future. It is no wonder that Isaiah has been so important in shaping the imagination of Christians. Isaiah is like a bridge between God's ancient promises to the people of Israel, and Jesus Christ and his church. For next time, we'll use that bridge to leap across time. Read Acts 1–2 ahead of time to prepare for the discussion.

Where (in what place, situation, or relationship) do you think God might be calling you to make a difference this week?

End the session by taking turns praying out loud together. Pray about the issues in your own lives. But be sure to include prayers for God's world, especially for those people who have a special place in God's heart...the poor, the outcast, those who are victims of injustice and prejudice, the forgotten. Pray that God would use you to make a difference for them.

7|WORKING TOGETHER

Being in partnership with God means being in partnership with one another.

COME AS YOU ARE

"Today," Jesus said, "a new king is in town!" In fact, there was a new KIND of king in town. (The last thing Israel needed was the OLD kind, after all.) In the kingdom Jesus was bringing, everyone would be invited to join the party. The hungry would be fed, the captive set free, the sinful forgiven. Those on the edges would be gathered in and given a seat at the head of the table. Everyone who needed it would have a new beginning. In Jesus' kingdom, the status quo would be challenged. The self-righteous and powerful would find themselves in the middle of a world turned upside down. No wonder Jesus ended up in such hot water. But being a new kind of king, not even death could get the best of him. God really *will* have the last word. And that is the good news Jesus shares with his followers right before he heads back to heaven. "It is now your job," he tells them, "to share the good news."

Spend some time checking in with each other, then pray together. It's your call, of course, on how to do this. If it hasn't already become your practice to do so, consider giving everyone a chance to pray out loud this time. When your turn comes, be sure to offer a prayer of thanks for something you have gotten out of being in this small group. When everybody finishes, pray this prayer together:

Surprising God, be with us now in our study. Let your Spirit be our guide. Help us see something new, hear something meaningful, and experience your power. In Jesus' name. Amen

JUST 3 QUESTIONS

Read Acts 1:1–2:21 out loud. Take turns reading a verse or two at a time. Then spend some time answering these three questions about the reading.

1 | **What do you think God is doing here?**

2 | **What do you hear God saying to you, personally?**

3 | **What do you hear God saying to us (as a small group, congregation, community, nation)?**

GROUP TIPS

COME AS YOU ARE

This is the last session in this No Experience Necessary unit. Your group may be feeling a little disappointed that Unit One is coming to an end. Or some may feel relieved! At any rate, your group should feel good about getting to this point. Spend a little time discussing what group members enjoyed the most about being in this small group.

If your group hasn't done this already, take some time to discuss reactions to the book *No Experience Necessary: Everybody's Welcome.*

JUST 3 QUESTIONS

Remember, this is the most important part of your time together. Don't rush through it—there is a lot going on in this reading. Take time to share your responses, listen, and learn from each other.

Our job description

GROUP TIPS

HEART OF THE MATTER

If necessary, take some time to silently read the lead article "Our Job Description." Then take a few minutes to talk about it. The questions at the end of the article might help get your conversation started.

When Jesus showed up in the Nazareth synagogue at the beginning of his ministry, he read from the book of Isaiah. This was his way of saying that his ministry was the continuation of something God had started long, long ago.

God created the world, of course. And God loves it. The world, and everyone in it, belongs to God! But from the beginning, people have been doing everything possible to mess it up. God's mission has been to bring this good but broken world back home again. This mission has been carried out, all along the way, by a cast of unlikely characters. These people—Abraham and Sarah, Moses and Miriam, Hannah and Samuel, and their descendants—were *the chosen* people. (If you need a reminder about how this all happened and what it means, revisit Session 3.) God had chosen to bless the whole world through them. And when (scripture-quoting, synagogue-attending, Sabbath-keeping) Jesus arrived on the scene, God could have said, "Promise kept! Case closed. Game over."

> **This mission has been carried out, all along the way, by a cast of unlikely characters.**

But, in some ways, things were just getting started.

A new day

When Jesus appeared, something happened that had never happened before. God showed up! And a new day dawned. God's kingdom came bursting in and the world was put on notice that nothing would ever be the same again. The blind could see. The lame could walk. The lepers were cleansed. The deaf could hear. The dead were raised. And the poor had good news brought to them. (This is how Jesus himself described what was happening. See Luke 7:22.) Lives were changed!

It was as if the doors to heaven swung open wide and the party *inside* spilled out into our world. Best of all, this was a party *everybody* was invited to. (In fact, Jesus uses this image in Luke 14:15-24, making it clear that he wanted his house to be filled!) You didn't have to be Jewish to join this party. You didn't have to be rich or smart. You didn't have to be a certain gender or sexual orientation or race. You didn't have to have a seminary degree or *any* degree! You didn't have to know all the right players or all the right prayers. You didn't have to have a perfect haircut or a perfect past. You didn't have to be perfect at all.

"The kingdom is yours," Jesus said. "You've lived it! Now go tell everybody else about it. And invite them to the party too!"

This is a weird kind of kingdom. It is so strange that Jesus resorted to all kinds of odd little stories, called *parables*, to help us get it. (See Luke 13:20-21, for example.) None of us would ever have dreamed it up. But here it was, in flesh and blood, in the face and the hands and the heart of Jesus Christ. Bringing in this kingdom is what Jesus himself said his ministry was all about (Luke 4:43). And in those last days before he went back to heaven, it was this kingdom that he told his disciples about (Acts 1:3). It was this kingdom that he gave to them.

Our job

"You will be my witnesses," Jesus told them (1:8). This implied that they had experienced the kingdom themselves. A witness doesn't tell facts about something. *A witness tells what he or she has seen and heard and felt.*

"The kingdom is yours," Jesus said. "You've lived it! Now go tell everybody else about it. And invite them to the party too!"

Obviously, there was still a lot of work to do. For starters, there were only 11 of them standing there—and they probably didn't feel much like talking about what happened to the twelfth (1:18-19). They knew very well that life was still too full of disappointment and death. They knew that too many people still walked in darkness, wandered homeless, and waited for freedom. They knew the world would resist their message and they would sometimes fight about it, even among themselves.

But this was their job. And Jesus promised that he would be with them (1:8).

"I will be right there with you in Spirit," he said. "And that will give you all the power you need."

Our mission and purpose

You couldn't call this little group a church, exactly. Not yet. Some say the church wasn't "born" until the day of Pentecost, when the Holy Spirit turned this group loose in the streets (Acts 2). Others argue this group became a church when they did what Jesus told them to do and finally left Jerusalem to take the good news to the rest of the world (8:4). But the job description Jesus gave them was *for the church*. When he said "you" will be my witnesses, he meant *all of you,* working together.

The whole rest of the story Luke tells here in Acts, his second book, is the story of how Jesus (through the Holy Spirit) helped his followers become the church they were called to be. He gave them an imagination for sharing the good news with people who were wildly different from them (Acts 8). He developed leaders from unlikely places (Acts 9). He challenged them when they insisted on doing things the way they'd always done them (Acts 15). He welcomed everyone (Acts 10). He empowered them when they stood up against the unjust powers of their day (Acts 4). He helped them see the gifts that everyone had to bring (16:11-15). He gave them courage to go where they had never gone before (Acts 20).

All these years later, Jesus is still at it. We are his witnesses today. There is no other mission for our congregations. There is no other mission for Christ's church.

There is no other purpose for our lives.

How would you describe the purpose of your life? How would you describe the mission of your congregation?

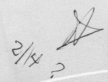

Eyes on the world

After Pentecost, the community of Christians grew like crazy. *Read Acts 2:37-47* right now for a description of what life among those early believers was like.

It was a wondrous time, a season of miracles. Perhaps the most miraculous thing of all was that these women and men "had all things in common" (2:44). They were together all the time, sharing their food and their lives.

> ## The main thing for those early Christians was the work they did "out there" in God's world.

What's interesting is that this is pretty much the last time life in the Christian community is described in this way. We see the community deliberating together (Acts 15) and trying to work out their disagreements (Acts 6). But we never, ever see them gathering for worship or small group Bible studies or evangelism committee meetings. They probably did these things. (Well, maybe not committee meetings!) But these were not the main things.

The main thing for those early Christians was the work they did "out there" in God's world. Jesus had given them these instructions: "You will be my witnesses in Jerusalem, in all Judea and Samaria, and to the ends of the earth" (1:8). And that's what they got busy doing. They knew the church was called, not just to gather, but to go.

Maybe that helps explain why the church was growing like crazy.

What would be different in your congregation if "going" was as important as "gathering"?

Pick one or two articles to talk about: "Eyes on the World," "Fighting Together," "A Different Angle," or "Lori." Use the questions at the end of the articles to get your conversation going.

Encourage group members to read the rest of the articles on their own during the week.

ANOTHER LOOK

If you choose this article, you'll read and discuss another portion of the Bible that sheds light on the main Bible passage.

Have everyone who is willing take turns reading a verse or two at a time from Acts 2:37-47.

It's helpful to know, as you're reading Luke–Acts, that this writer believes the Christian church is living in the "between times." We are between Jesus' ministry on earth and the time when he will come again. We can't know or predict when that end will come. We aren't even supposed to wonder about it (Acts 1:7)! But we do know what our job is in the meantime. We are to be Christ's witnesses (1:8), trusting in his promise to always be with us.

Fighting together

After the Spirit showed up on Pentecost, Jesus' followers got right to work. And it wasn't long before trouble started. *Read Acts 4:1-22* to see what happened.

Peter and John found themselves in the middle of conflict. In this case, their conflict was with the religious leaders of their community, the teachers and priests and administrators of the temple. These leaders didn't like the message Peter and John were delivering, the commotion they caused wherever they showed up, or the fact that people were so interested in what they had to say. Now, to be sure, Peter and John weren't looking for trouble. Certainly they would have liked nothing more than to have the support of the religious leaders. How much easier that would have made their job! But they answered to a higher authority. "We're very sorry," they said. "But we have to listen to God."

Besides, they had to have known that conflict came with the job.

The book of Acts is full of stories like this. Those early Christians found themselves in conflict with the governmental authorities (17:1-9), local merchants (19:21-41), and townspeople (Acts 7). They even got each other pretty upset from time to time, as they disagreed about the direction the Spirit seemed to be leading them (Acts 15).

God's people are called to live like a new kingdom has arrived. In this new kingdom, there is no king except Jesus. Blessings are meant to be given away.

> ## Conflict can help us see the direction God wants us to go, motivate us to think creatively, and inspire us to act courageously.

There are no lines dividing us from each other. Everyone has gifts to share. And "the way we've always done it" is no longer a legitimate reason to do anything. Conflict is inevitable! Jesus' own life—and death—was proof of that.

The question isn't "Can we avoid conflict?" The biblical story tells us conflict is part of following Jesus. The question is "Can anything good come out of it?" And the answer is a definite "Yes!"

In the book of Acts, even the most serious conflicts often led to good outcomes. Gentiles (*JEN-tiles*, referring to everyone who wasn't Jewish) were included in the ministry of the early church (Acts 11; 15). New models of leadership were developed (6:1-7). The good news got carried beyond Jerusalem (8:1-4) and spread to distant regions (15:36-41).

According to Acts, conflict is an inevitable part of being the church. And because the Holy Spirit is in the mix, good things often come from it. Conflict can help us see the direction God wants us to go, motivate us to think creatively, and inspire us to act courageously. Conflict can be good!

So how come we sometimes seem so afraid of it?

What *potential* conflict is on the horizon for your congregation? What can you do to help members embrace the possibility that this conflict could lead to something good?

A different angle

People from all over the ancient world were in Jerusalem for Pentecost, a celebration of the harvest. The Spirit could have made everyone understand Aramaic (a dialect of Hebrew, the language those early Christians probably spoke), but, instead, it gave Jesus' followers the ability to speak in *many different* languages.

We are called to work together, but God is not interested in making us all the same. God honors our languages, our experiences, our unique contexts, and the communities where we actually live our lives. Part of working together is learning to appreciate those differences too.

Do you hear what I hear?

One of the differences between those of us who live in Western nations and Christians in other parts of the world is in the way we read the Bible. For example, in our part of the world, the book of Acts has traditionally been read as a story about how the apostles set up the church. The idea has been that our job is to maintain the church they started. When it came to the story of Matthias (Acts 1:23-26), we said, "See that? The church needs leaders. And leaders should look like Matthias."

Christians in other parts of the world, especially those who are very poor, hear this story differently. Frankly, in many places (especially in Latin America), the church has not always been very tuned in to the needs of the poor. In some cases, church leaders have worked on the side of unjust governments *against* the poor. For people living in these places, the book of Acts looks like a story about the Holy Spirit.

One Latin American scholar (Justo Gonzalez, writing in *Acts: The Gospel of the Spirit*) actually says the book of Acts should be known as the *Acts of the Spirit*, not The Acts of the Apostles. And in the case of Matthias, Gonzalez points out how he *disappears* from the book of Acts after this story. Maybe that's because the way he was chosen wasn't exactly Spirit-led. Maybe this story isn't meant to be an example for us to follow, Gonzalez suggests, but a warning!

From this Latin American perspective, the Spirit gets center stage. The point is that today we can still be open to the Spirit. The Spirit leads us to confront distorted values and oppressive practices in society, Gonzalez argues, and to confront the church whenever hierarchy, privilege, and tradition become more important than being a part of God's mission.

Honoring differences

There's nothing like looking at things from a different angle to get us thinking, listening for God's voice through the ears of somebody different from us, and sharing what we are hearing, from our perspective. We can learn a lot from each other that way. Maybe that's what God was up to on that Pentecost day.

Maybe God was *making sure* we'd all be different.

Who are you? Where are you from? Can you see how your experiences shape the way you read the biblical stories?

GROUP TIPS

RIGHT TO THE POINT

If you choose this article, you'll focus on one key thing about God and following Jesus.

Take turns reading Acts 4:1-22.

BIBLE BASICS

If you choose this article, you'll learn more about the Bible and listening for what God is saying through these words.

Lori

Lori was raised in a churchgoing family but, for a lot of reasons, she hadn't had a relationship with the church (much less with God) for a really long time. Her life had taken more than a few sharp turns. When she walked into our worship service for the first time, it was because she had been invited by some friends who thought we might have something she needed. We did. But she was scared. She was afraid of not fitting in, of being judged.

Lori taught me a lot in the years that followed about what people "out there" think about those of us "in here." She helped me see how "church people" look to people who, for whatever reason, are not part of a Christian faith community. We have a variety of rituals they don't totally understand (if at all!) and traditions that mean nothing to them. We speak a different language. What's worse, we don't always seem very interested in learning their language or finding out what is important to them.

But Lori also helped me realize that what we have—the good news of God's love for the world, through Jesus Christ—is exactly what the world needs. The good news helped heal her. It gave her life a whole new direction. In all kinds of unexpected and wonderful ways, it set her free.

Now Lori is a worship leader in that congregation. Together, she and I are part of a team that helps other congregations across the country share the good news with the people in their communities. She writes songs and lets God use her amazing voice to inspire us all to, as she puts it, "Love all those people out there who are just like me." She smiles when she says this because, well, she knows just how hard that can be.

But she also knows this: That's our job.

What we have—the good news of God's love for the world, through Jesus Christ—is exactly what the world needs.

Who are the people in your community who especially need what you have? As the Spirit stirs in your heart (and in your congregation), who are you being called to reach out to in love?

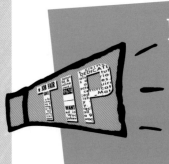

The same person wrote both The Gospel of Luke and the book of Acts. That's why Acts 1:1 starts out saying, "In the first book…" We can't know for sure who wrote these books or when. We know the writer wasn't an eyewitness to the events recorded here (Luke 1:1-4), but based Luke and Acts on accounts given by those who were. The work of others was also used, but it seems the writer didn't think their books were very well done (Luke 1:3)!

GET GOING

Wrap up

The book of Acts, in some ways, is where our story really begins. We are living in the "between times." When Jesus came, something happened that had never happened before! God showed up and the party began. Our job now is to invite the world to join us. That is the purpose of our lives and of our congregations. It is what it means to be the church. We are called to be a part of what God is up to in this world, to witness and serve and love and give ourselves away. We are God's partners in mission until that day when the kingdom, finally, comes.

How have you been changed by this Bible study experience?

Pray out loud together. Go around the group and take turns saying thank-you prayers for each other. Ask for God's blessings as you go on the adventure God has in store for each of you.

GROUP TIPS

RIGHT HERE, RIGHT NOW

If you choose this article, you'll read about real people becoming involved in God's mission to bless and save the world.

GET GOING

Read "Wrap Up" out loud or silently. Then take turns answering the question.

What is God calling you and your group to do now? Some will want to take a break from being part of a Bible study group. Others will want to begin Unit Two right away! A few might start a new group and invite NEW people to join them. Honor each person's decision.

Try holding hands during the closing prayer. After the prayer, if you'd like, have each person make the sign of the cross on the forehead of the person on her or his left, as a way of blessing each other. (Using your index finger, "draw" a vertical line, then a horizontal line intersecting it, to form a simple cross.)

BIBLIOGRAPHY

Brueggemann, Walter. *Isaiah 1–39* (Westminster Bible Companion series). Louisville, Kentucky: Westminster John Knox Press, 1998. (Session 6)

Childs, Brevard S. *Isaiah* (The Old Testament Library). Louisville, Kentucky: Westminster John Knox Press, 2001. (Session 6)

Craddock, Fred B. *Luke (Interpretation: A Bible Commentary for Teaching and Preaching).* Louisville, Kentucky: Westminster John Knox Press, 1991. (Session 1)

Fretheim, Terence E. *Exodus (Interpretation: A Bible Commentary for Teaching and Preaching).* Louisville, Kentucky: Westminster John Knox Press, 1991. (Session 4)

Fretheim, Terence E. *The Pentateuch.* Nashville: Abingdon Press, 1996. (Sessions 2, 3, 4)

González, Justo L. *Acts: The Gospel of the Spirit.* Maryknoll, New York: Orbis Books, 2001. (Session 7)

Janzen, J. Gerald. *Exodus* (Westminster Bible Companion series). Louisville, Kentucky: Westminster John Knox Press, 1997. (Session 4)

Mays, James Luther and Paul J. Achtemeier, editors. *Interpreting the Prophets.* Philadelphia: Fortress Press, 1987. (Session 6)

McCarter Jr., P. Kyle. *I Samuel: A New Translation with Introduction and Commentary* (The Anchor Bible). New York: Doubleday, 1980. (Session 5)

Meeks, Wayne, editor. *The HarperCollins Study Bible: New Revised Standard Version.* New York: HarperSanFrancisco, 1993. (Sessions 4, 5)

Metzger, Bruce M. and Michael Coogan, editors. *The Oxford Guide to People & Places of the Bible.* New York: Oxford University Press, 2001. (Sessions 2, 3, 5)

Nolland, John. *Word Biblical Commentary 35A: Luke 1–9:20.* Dallas: Word, Incorporated, 1989. (Session 1)

Propp, William, H. C. *Exodus 1–18: A New Translation with Introduction and Commentary* (The Anchor Bible). New York: Doubleday, 1999. (Session 4)

Seitz, Christopher R. *Isaiah 1–39 (Interpretation: A Bible Commentary for Teaching and Preaching).* Louisville, Kentucky: Westminster John Knox Press, 1993. (Session 6)

Stumme, Wayne (editor). *Bible and Mission.* Minneapolis: Augsburg, 1986; out of print. (Session 3)

Wenham, Gordon J. *Word Biblical Commentary 1: Genesis 1–15.* Dallas: Word, Incorporated, 1987. (Sessions 2, 3)

Willimon, William H. *Acts (Interpretation: A Bible Commentary for Teaching and Preaching).* Louisville, Kentucky: Westminster John Knox Press, 1988. (Session 7)

Wold, Margaret. *Women of Faith and Spirit: Profiles of Fifteen Biblical Witnesses.* Minneapolis: Augsburg, 1987; out of print. (Sessions 3, 4)